sugar + spice cookies

sugar + spice cookies

creative recipes *for* home baking

megan neveu

PAGE STREET
PUBLISHING CO.

PAGE STREET
PUBLISHING CO.

First published in 2022 by
Page Street Publishing Co.
27 Congress Street, Suite 1511
Salem, MA 01970
www.pagestreetpublishing.com

Distributed by Macmillan, sales in Canada by The Canadian Manda Group.

26   25   24   23   22   1   2   3   4   5

ISBN-13: 978-1-64567-718-5
ISBN-10: 1-64567-718-4

Library of Congress Control Number: 2022940182

Cover and book design by Megan Neveu
Photography by Megan Neveu

Printed and bound in the United States of America

to o + t, the loves of my life

TABLE OF CONTENTS

introduction

Hi and welcome to *Sugar + Spice Cookies*, where unique and nuanced flavors from spices and herbs come alive in each sugary bite of cookie bliss. My love for infusing fresh flavor combinations into classic sweet treats can be found in many recipes on my blog, Olives + Thyme. While I love all things sweet, my love of cookies knows no bounds. *Sugar + Spice Cookies* brings together my two passions: fun flavor pairings and classic cookies.

As a home baker, I have written this book as a source of inspiration and joy for other home bakers who love to try fun and creative cookie recipes. Like all things in life, I find that baking is part following the process and part trusting yourself and your senses. For the novice baker, use these recipes to become familiar with the process of making and baking cookies. Remember, every experienced baker was once a novice. For the more experienced baker, use these recipes as a guide and a jumping-off point in creating your own favorite versions of these cookies. Most important, take these recipes as an invitation to play and have fun in the kitchen.

In this book, you will find recipes that take spices and herbs such as cinnamon and ginger or lavender and rosemary and pair them with classic cookie bases such as sugar and chocolate chip. The result is fun and fresh flavor combinations that will make your senses come alive. I hope that each one you try becomes your new favorite cookie.

This book is divided into five chapters, each with its own personality and flavor focus.

Classics is like an embrace from an old friend. It's warm, familiar and comforting. The recipes in the Classics chapter use lots of warming spices such as cinnamon, ginger, cardamom, nutmeg and cloves. In this chapter, you will find classic cookies with a creative spin such as Coffee Cake (page 17), Apple Spice Cinnamon Roll (page 18) and Pumpkin Snicker-doodle Cookie Sandwiches (page 27). These are the cookies you reach for when you need something cozy to share with loved ones.

Chocolate is exactly as the name implies: lots and lots of chocolate! If you're like me, you already know who you will bake these cookies for. In this chapter, you will find recipes that utilize spice blends such as chai and pumpkin to enhance and bring out the more nuanced flavors of this beloved roasted bean. From Tahini Chocolate Chip (page 51) to Tiramisu Brownie Cookies (page 52), these are the recipes you will go to for your next chocolate craving.

Nuts is designed to celebrate the buttery, creamy and earthy quality of your favorite nuts. Sweet spices such as cinnamon pair beautifully with citrus and toasted pecans in my Spiced Mexican Wedding Cookies (page 84), while buttery shortbread provides the perfect base for a sweet and salty caramelized honey nut filling in Salted Honey Nut Bars (page 94).

Herbs brings the bright and tart flavors of lemon, orange and lime and pairs them with floral, sweet and woodsy herbs such as lavender, thyme, rosemary and mint. In this chapter, you will find classic pairings such as lemon and thyme, as well as more modern flavor pairings such as lavender and chocolate in the Lavender Brownie Cookies (page 108) and rosemary and chocolate in the Rosemary Oatmeal Chocolate Chip cookies (page 112).

Fruit is filled with spiced cookies that are designed to highlight the scents and flavors of fresh fruit. This chapter features recipes such as Raspberry Cardamom cookies (page 133), a chai-spiced Mixed Berry Skillet Cookie (page 134) and Banana Peanut Butter Cup cookies (page 147). These recipes pair cardamom, chai and coriander (yes, coriander) with fresh berries, bananas and apples for the most delicious fruit-forward cookies.

Thank you for bringing *Sugar + Spice Cookies* into your home. It is truly an honor and a privilege to share my love of baking with you. Happy baking, friends.

my best tips for cookie baking, ingredients and tools

BEFORE YOU BEGIN

Make sure you carefully read through the _entire_ recipe before beginning. Go through the ingredient list and make a grocery list to buy any of the ingredients you don't have on hand. Next, read through the instructions to get a sense of which tools you need. Also keep in mind that some cookies will require a longer chilling time, so it's good to note this before starting a recipe.

Bring ingredients to room temperature, unless written otherwise. Room temperature ingredients mix together better than cold ingredients, resulting in a better-tasting cookie. **In a pinch, eggs and butter can quickly be brought to room temperature.** Place the whole egg(s) into a bowl or large cup filled with very warm water for 1 minute. For butter, slice it into tablespoon-sized (14-g) pieces, and lay each piece flat at room temperature for 20 to 30 minutes.

Measure out ingredients at the start for a seamless baking experience. Each recipe lists the ingredients by volume and weight. A digital food scale is an easy-to-use tool that comes in handy when baking. After an initial read through the recipe, my "mise en place" routine begins by preheating the oven and pulling out all my cold ingredients. During this time, I slice my butter to bring it to room temperature quickly. If I need to divide an egg to use just the yolk, I do this while it's still cold and easier to divide. I then measure out all my dry ingredients into a bowl using a food scale and do a thorough whisk to combine. Once that's finished, I will measure or pull out any sugars, extracts and mix-ins needed for the recipe. Usually, by the time all this is done, the butter and eggs have reached room temperature, and I can begin to make the cookies.

Preheat the oven early. Many ovens need at least 25 to 30 minutes to fully preheat before the internal temperature truly matches the temperature on the digital panel.

MAKING THE COOKIES

Mix the dough until the dry ingredients are just combined with the wet. Overmixing can result in a tougher, drier cookie.

Chilling the dough is always recommended for the best-tasting cookie. Chilling the dough allows the gluten to rest and the dough to hydrate. Sometimes this step is essential to the structure of the cookie. Other times, it's done for a more flavorful cookie. Either way, the recipe will note when it is important to chill the dough to get the best results in that particular cookie. Make sure to always wrap or cover the dough completely with plastic wrap. Unless stated otherwise in the recipe, I recommend allowing the dough to sit out at room temperature for 20 to 30 minutes prior to baking if the dough has been chilling for 2 or more hours.

Reserve some chocolate chips or chunks for topping cookies right before baking. As the cookies bake, these extra chocolate pieces melt beautifully on top, creating photo-worthy cookies.

AFTER THE COOKIES BAKE

For perfectly round cookies, take a round cookie cutter, pastry ring or other round object that is slightly wider than the cookie. Place the cookie cutter over the cookie, with the edges of the cookie on the inside of the cookie cutter. Gently nudge the edges of the cookie in a circular motion back into a round shape. This is best done the first few minutes the cookies come out of the oven, while they are still on the baking sheets.

Completely cool the cookies to room temperature before adding any glazes or frostings.

INGREDIENT NOTES

all-purpose flour

Also known as plain flour, all-purpose flour is the most commonly used type for baking cookies. Look for a protein content of 10 to 12 percent if you aren't sure which flour type you have in your pantry. Measure flour by using a food scale or by scooping spoonfuls of flour into a measuring cup and leveling off any excess from the top using a straightedge such as a butter knife. One cup of all-purpose flour weighs 120 to 128 grams.

butter

All the recipes in this book use uncultured, unsalted (sweet cream) butter. Many recipes in this book call for room-temperature butter. This butter is cool to the touch, but a finger pressed into the surface will leave an indentation in the butter. It should not slide off or sink in. If you have a digital thermometer, the butter should read 65°F (18°C).

Some of the recipes call for brown butter. This is simply unsalted butter that has been melted in a pan long enough for the milk solids in the butter to brown. The result is a melted butter that smells nutty and very fragrant. Using brown butter in a recipe brings another depth of flavor. It also adds a bit more fat and less water content to the overall recipe. Any recipe where brown butter is used adds 2 tablespoons (28 g) of butter per ½ cup (113 g) of butter to account for the loss of water. If you would like to skip the step of browning the butter, simply omit the extra 2 tablespoons (28 g) per ½ cup (113 g) of butter.

buttermilk

A quick DIY version of this can be made by pouring 1 tablespoon (15 ml) of white vinegar or lemon juice into a 1-cup (240-ml) measuring cup. Fill the rest of the cup with milk. Gently stir the mixture and allow it to sit and curdle for 10 minutes.

cake flour

This flour is finer and softer than all-purpose flour, with a lower protein content of 7 to 9 percent. As the name suggests, this flour is commonly used to produce a more cake-like consistency in baked goods. If you don't have cake flour on hand, it's really easy to make at home. Simply take 1 cup (120 g) of all-purpose flour and scoop out 2 tablespoons (16 g). Replace the 2 tablespoons with 2 tablespoons (20 g) of cornstarch or cornflower and sift the new mixture together three times to fully combine.

eggs

All the recipes in this book use U.S. large eggs at a weight of 57 grams per egg.

nut flours

I love baking with a blend of nut flour and all-purpose flour. Typically I like to use ¼ to ½ cup (weight varies) of a nut flour blended with all-purpose flour for a chewier cookie. For almost all recipes in this book, the nut flour can be substituted with the same weight of all-purpose flour. For example, ¼ cup of almond flour weighs 28 grams. This can be replaced with ¼ cup (30 g) of all-purpose flour. To make your own nut flour, simply place the nuts in a food processor and process until the nuts are a sand-like consistency.

spices

Ground spices and fresh herbs are central to all the recipes in this cookie book. Make sure to use fresh spices or spice blends for the best-tasting cookies. If you can't find fresh herbs, 1 teaspoon of dried herbs can be used in place of 1 tablespoon (weight varies) of fresh herbs.

SPECIAL TOOLS AND EQUIPMENT

baking sheets

I always have two 13 x 18–inch (33 x 46–cm) baking sheets ready to go when baking a batch of cookies. If you're working with just one baking sheet, allow the cookies to cool on the hot baking sheet for the length of time written in the recipe. Transfer the cookies to a cooling rack to cool further. Remove the parchment paper from the pan, and run the entire pan under cold water for about 30 seconds. Once cooled, dry the pan, replace the parchment paper and *voila*, the pan is ready for the next batch of cookies!

cast-iron skillet

The skillet cookies in this book were developed using a 9-inch (23-cm) cast-iron skillet. However, the same recipes will also bake well in a 10-inch (25-cm) cast-iron skillet. Please note that the baking times will shift slightly as the larger skillet bakes a thinner cookie. I recommend checking the cookie for doneness about 5 minutes before the time listed in the recipe if you're using a 10-inch (25-cm) cast-iron skillet.

conventional oven vs. convection oven

All the recipes for this book have been developed using a conventional oven. This is an oven without a fan. If you are baking on a convection/fan oven, I recommend reducing the baking temperature by 25°F. In other words, if a recipe calls for a baking temperature of 375°F (190°C), the convection/fan oven temperature should be reduced to 350°F (180°C) and baked for the same length of time as written in the recipe.

cookie scoops

This is a tool that I use again and again in my kitchen. Cookie scoops provide perfectly portioned cookies every time. For this book, I use a small cookie scoop for 1-tablespoon (15-g) cookies, medium for 2-tablespoon (30-g) cookies and large for 3-tablespoon (45-g) cookies. These are completely optional, but they do make a big difference in creating perfect-looking cookies. It's worth it to pick up a set if you bake cookies often.

food processor

This is used most often for grinding nuts into an almond flour consistency. If you have one, it definitely makes the work of finely chopping nuts much faster. If you don't have one, I recommend buying the nut flour or just get ready for lots of chopping.

large cookie cutters or pastry rings

Use these to help reshape freshly baked cookies so they look perfectly round. See "After the Cookies Bake" on page 10 for how to reshape a cookie.

metal/aluminum pans

I prefer to use metal pans made out of aluminum when baking cookie bars. I love the crisp corners and straight edges. If you use glass pans to bake the cookie bars, I recommend reducing the oven temperature by 25°F and baking for the same time listed in the recipe.

oven thermometer

This is one of the cheapest and most-used tools in my kitchen. I highly recommend hanging one inside the middle of your oven to ensure the correct baking temperature. Many ovens can run either too hot or too cold. This tool helps ensure your cookies are baking at the proper temperature. It's also an easy way to double-check your oven has fully preheated. If you find that your cookies bake unevenly, you can also use your oven thermometer to help identify hot spots in the oven. Place the oven thermometer in different areas of your oven to see if the temperature changes. Use that knowledge to adjust your baking process, such as rotating the baking sheet midway through baking.

parchment paper

I highly recommend lining baking sheets and baking pans with parchment paper. This promotes even baking and makes cleaning up a breeze. A reusable nonstick baking mat also works well.

piping bags and tips

There is only one recipe in the book (Churro Cookies on page 33) where a specific piping tip is required. If you are an avid baker, use your preferred tip and pastry bag. Otherwise, fill a ziplock bag with the frosting or filling and cut off the corner to fill or top cookies with the fillings and frosting.

stand mixer

As someone who bakes for a living, I always turn to my trusty stand mixer. You'll find the recipes in this book call for a stand mixer with a paddle or whisk attachment. Rest assured that an electric hand mixer will work in place of a stand mixer. Just keep in mind that the mixing times may differ slightly as hand mixers are less powerful than stand mixers.

Don't have an electric mixer? No problem! You'll need a wooden spoon, fork and lots of arm strength to cream the butter and sugar effectively. Place the softened butter and sugar into a large mixing bowl. Thoroughly mash the butter and sugar together with the wooden spoon. If the butter isn't softened enough to work into the sugar, you can use your hands to work it in, similar to working butter into flour for a pie crust. Once the butter and sugar are thoroughly mixed together, use a fork to whip in some air. Use a motion similar to the way you would scramble eggs. Whip the butter and sugar together until there are no visible pieces of butter. This can take 5 minutes of continuous whipping. The end result should be creamy, lump free and lighter in color.

zester

This comes in handy when zesting citrus fruits. I love using a Microplane® zester. If needed, you can also use the smallest holes on a box grater. If using a box grater, be careful to zest only the lightest top layer of the citrus fruit and not the white pith underneath, which will make the zest taste more bitter.

Classics
warm and cozy

Although this entire book is created around sweet and spice-filled cookies, this chapter is dedicated to the warming spices you know and love. Warming spices are a group of spices such as cinnamon, ginger, cloves, cardamom and nutmeg that have both a physical and emotional warming effect on the body. Simply writing out the words "pumpkin spice" instantly fills my mind with autumn leaves, scarves and warm lattes shared with friends on cool, crisp mornings. This happens because our minds and bodies are finely tuned to the changing seasons and therefore crave spices that wholly warm and nourish us. Although these cookies can and should be made year-round, they are particularly perfect for the colder months of the year when your body is craving something warm and inviting.

Some recipes in this chapter require a bit of time and preparation, such as the Apple Cider Sugar cookies (page 38), while others, such as the Cinnamon Cereal cookies (page 24) come together as quickly as you can mix the dough.

coffee cake

makes 16 cookies

These cookies take all my favorite parts of coffee cake and reimagine them as giant, cozy cookies. The scents of warming spices and the textures of cake and crumble topping invoke the feeling of warmth and connection. I intentionally chose this cookie as the first recipe in the book as an invitation for you to pull up a chair, grab a cup of coffee or tea and find the cookie recipes you most want to share with the people you love.

INGREDIENTS

for the spiced streusel topping

½ cup (60 g) all-purpose flour

½ cup (100 g) light brown sugar

2 tsp (6 g) ground cinnamon

¼ cup (60 ml) melted unsalted butter

for the coffee cake cookies

1½ cups (180 g) all-purpose flour

1¼ cups (150 g) cake flour

2 tsp (6 g) ground cinnamon

1 tsp ground ginger

½ tsp baking powder

¼ tsp baking soda

½ tsp salt

1 cup (226 g) unsalted butter, room temperature

1½ cups (300 g) light brown sugar

1 large egg, room temperature

1 large egg yolk, room temperature

2 tsp (10 ml) vanilla bean paste or vanilla extract

for the vanilla bean glaze

1 cup (120 g) confectioners' sugar

1 tsp vanilla bean paste

1 tbsp (15 ml) milk, plus more as needed

DIRECTIONS

Preheat the oven to 375°F (190°C). Line two large baking sheets with parchment paper.

To make the streusel topping, in a medium mixing bowl, whisk together the flour, brown sugar and cinnamon until well combined. Pour half of the melted butter over the dry ingredients. With a fork, drag the butter through the dry ingredients until mostly combined. Pour in the remaining melted butter and continue incorporating the butter until the mixture resembles coarse, wet sand. Set the streusel in the fridge until it's time to top the cookies.

To make the cookies, in a medium bowl, whisk together both flours, the cinnamon, ground ginger, baking powder, baking soda and salt until well combined. In the bowl of a stand mixer fitted with the paddle attachment, cream the butter and sugar together on medium speed for 3 minutes, or until well combined. Scrape the bottom and sides of the bowl as needed. On low speed, mix in the egg, egg yolk and vanilla bean paste until smooth and well combined. Scrape the bottom and sides of the bowl as needed. On low speed or by hand, mix the dry ingredients into the wet until just combined.

Scoop 3-tablespoon (45-g) amounts of the cookie dough onto the baking sheets, spacing them 3 inches (8 cm) apart. Using the palm of your hand, gently flatten the tops of the cookie dough balls till they are ½ inch (1.3 cm) thick. Top each cookie with a heaping tablespoon (17 g) of streusel. Gently press the streusel into the top of the cookie. Bake the cookies for 12 to 14 minutes, or until the edges of the cookies set. Keep the cookies on the hot baking sheets for 5 minutes before transferring them to a cooling rack to cool for 30 minutes.

While the cookies cool, make the vanilla bean glaze. In a medium mixing bowl, add the sugar. Mix in the vanilla bean paste and 1 tablespoon (15 ml) of the milk until smooth and well combined. If needed, add 1 to 3 teaspoons (5 to 15 ml) of additional milk. Drizzle the vanilla bean glaze on top of the cooled cookies. Allow the glaze to set for 15 to 20 minutes before serving.

apple spice cinnamon roll

makes 28 cookies

Cinnamon rolls are the quintessential cozy breakfast food. They are in season every time of the year, and these are a fun take on this classic comfort food. The soft sugar cookie base features a buttery, cinnamon-spiced filling, making them look and taste just like cinnamon rolls. Top them with a maple glaze for the ultimate cozy cookie experience.

INGREDIENTS

for the cinnamon roll cookies

2¼ cups (270 g) all-purpose flour

½ cup (56 g) almond flour

2 tsp (6 g) apple pie spice

¾ tsp baking powder

½ tsp salt

1 cup (226 g) unsalted butter, room temperature

1 cup (200 g) light brown sugar

1 large egg, room temperature

1½ tsp (8 ml) vanilla extract

for the cinnamon filling

6 tbsp (90 ml) melted unsalted butter

1 tbsp (9 g) ground cinnamon

¾ cup (150 g) light brown sugar

DIRECTIONS

To make the cookies, in a medium mixing bowl, whisk together the all-purpose flour, almond flour, apple pie spice, baking powder and salt until well combined. In the bowl of a stand mixer fitted with the paddle attachment, beat the butter and sugar together on medium speed for 3 to 4 minutes, or until light, fluffy and well combined. Scrape the bottom and sides of the bowl. On low speed, mix in the egg and vanilla until well combined. Scrape the bottom and sides of the bowl. Mix together at low speed for 30 seconds. On low speed or by hand, mix the dry ingredients into the wet until just combined.

Roughly divide the dough into two sections. Place one dough ball onto a lightly floured piece of parchment paper. Place another piece of parchment paper on top of the dough. Roll the dough into a ¼-inch (6-mm)-thick rectangle. Repeat with the remaining cookie dough on another piece of parchment paper. Transfer the rectangles onto a small baking sheet or large plate. Place in the fridge to chill for a few minutes while you make the filling.

To make the filling, add the butter to a small mixing bowl. Stir in the cinnamon and sugar until well combined.

Remove the rectangles from the fridge. Spread one half of the filling onto each of the rectangles. Using the parchment paper as a guide, roll the rectangles into logs. Place each log back onto the baking sheet or large plate. Loosely cover the dough with plastic wrap. Chill it in the fridge for 1 to 2 hours, or until the dough is firm.

(continued)

apple spice cinnamon roll (continued)

for the maple glaze
1½ cups (180 g) confectioners' sugar

2 tbsp (30 ml) maple syrup

½ tsp vanilla extract

1 tbsp (15 ml) milk, plus more as needed

Preheat the oven to 350°F (180°C). Line a baking sheet with parchment paper.

Remove the dough from the fridge. Slice the logs into ½-inch (1.3-cm) round cookies. Place each cookie onto the baking sheet, spacing them 2 inches (5 cm) apart. Bake for 11 to 12 minutes, or until the edges are set and lightly golden brown. Keep the cookies on the hot baking sheet for 5 minutes before transferring them to a cooling rack to cool completely.

To make the glaze, in a small bowl, whisk together the confectioners' sugar, maple syrup, vanilla and 1 tablespoon (15 ml) of milk until well combined. If needed, add up to 1 tablespoon (15 ml) of additional milk. Drizzle the glaze over the cooled cookies. Allow the glaze to set for 30 to 45 minutes before serving.

chai carrot cake cookie sandwiches

makes 12–14 cookie sandwiches

For years, the most popular recipe on my blog has been my chai carrot loaf cake. Inspired by how loved that loaf cake is, I decided to make a cookie version that's just as cozy and delicious. These cookies are made from a generously spiced, chewy oatmeal cookie dough that's filled with finely shredded carrots. Although wonderfully delicious on their own, these cookies are even better when sandwiched together with the brown butter and cream cheese frosting. These cookies require a bit of planning, but they are more than worth the wait.

INGREDIENTS

for the brown butter

1¾ cups + 2 tbsp (424 g) unsalted butter (see tip)

for the chai carrot cake cookies

1½ cups (180 g) all-purpose flour

1 tsp baking soda

½ tsp ground cinnamon

½ tsp ground cardamom

½ tsp ground ginger

¼ tsp ground cloves

¼ tsp ground nutmeg

½ tsp salt

1 cup (226 g) prepared brown butter, softened but cold

¾ cup (150 g) light brown sugar

¾ cup (150 g) granulated sugar

1 large egg, room temperature

1 large egg yolk, room temperature

2 tsp (10 ml) vanilla extract

1 cup (110 g) finely shredded carrots

2½ cups (215 g) old-fashioned or rolled oats

DIRECTIONS

To make the brown butter, melt the butter in a heavy bottom saucepan over medium heat for 7 to 10 minutes, or until the butter starts to foam. Whisk continuously until brown bits start to form. Depending on your stove and saucepan, the entire process should take 10 to 15 minutes. Immediately remove the pan from the heat, and pour the brown butter into a clean bowl to cool for 30 minutes, or until it reaches room temperature. Measure out the liquid brown butter into two containers. One should measure 1 cup (240 ml) for the cookie dough, and the other will measure ½ cup (120 ml) for the frosting. Transfer the containers to the fridge to solidify for 1½ to 2 hours, or until the butter reaches a softened texture.

To make the sandwich cookies, in a medium mixing bowl, whisk together the flour, baking soda, cinnamon, cardamom, ginger, cloves, nutmeg and salt. In the bowl of a stand mixer fitted with the paddle attachment, cream the 1 cup (240 ml) of brown butter, light brown sugar and granulated sugar on medium speed for 3 minutes, or until well combined. Add the egg, egg yolk and vanilla, one at a time, beating on low for 20 seconds before adding the next. On low, mix in the shredded carrots. On the lowest mixing speed or by hand, stir the dry ingredients into the wet until just combined. Stir in the oats until just combined. Cover the cookie dough with plastic wrap. Chill it in the fridge for 1 to 2 hours and up to overnight. Pull cookies out of the fridge 10 minutes before you want to start baking them.

Preheat the oven to 375°F (190°C). Line a large baking sheet with parchment paper.

(continued)

chai carrot cake cookie sandwiches (continued)

for the brown butter and cream cheese frosting

½ cup (113 g) prepared brown butter, softened but cold

4 oz (113 g) cream cheese, room temperature

2½ cups (310 g) sifted confectioners' sugar

1 tsp vanilla extract

¼ tsp salt

1 tbsp (15 ml) milk, plus more as needed

Scoop 1-tablespoon (15-g) amounts of the cookie dough and roll them into balls with your hands. Place them on the baking sheet, spacing them 3 inches (8 cm) apart. The cookies will spread while baking. Bake for 10 to 12 minutes, or until golden brown around the edges and slightly underbaked (and a little puffed) in the center. Keep the cookies on the hot baking sheet for 10 minutes before transferring them to a cooling rack to cool completely before adding the frosting.

While the cookies cool, make the frosting. In the bowl of a stand mixer fitted with the paddle attachment, cream the softened brown butter with the cream cheese for 4 to 5 minutes, or until creamy and well combined. Scrape the bottom and sides of the bowl as needed. On low, beat in the sifted confectioners' sugar, ½ cup (60 g) at a time. Scrape the bottom and sides of the bowl as needed. Mix in the vanilla, salt and milk. Beat on medium speed until the mixture is fully incorporated and your desired consistency. If the frosting is too thick, mix in an additional 1 to 2 tablespoons (15 to 30 ml) of milk.

To assemble, apply your desired amount of frosting to the bottom of one cookie. Place the bottom of another cookie to the frosted side of the first cookie and gently press together.

tip: Make the brown butter the day before or 2 to 3 hours before you plan to make the cookies.

cinnamon cereal

makes 20 cookies

Growing up, one of my favorite cereals was Cinnamon Toast Crunch™. It was the perfect way to start my day. There was something so simple and delicious about that crunchy, cinnamon-sugar taste. Plus, it made the milk taste incredible. These cookies are my wink and nod to my favorite childhood cereal. They're sweet, buttery, cinnamon-spiced cookies that are reminiscent of both a soft sugar cookie and a snickerdoodle. Top these with a drizzle of creamy, cinnamony glaze for the most delicious cereal-inspired cookie!

INGREDIENTS

for the cinnamon cereal cookies

2 cups (80 g) square cinnamon cereal

2 cups (240 g) all-purpose flour

2 tsp (6 g) ground cinnamon

½ tsp baking soda

½ tsp baking powder

½ tsp salt

1 cup (226 g) unsalted butter, room temperature

1 cup (200 g) granulated sugar

1 large egg, room temperature

1 large egg yolk

2 tsp (10 ml) vanilla extract

for the cinnamon cereal milk glaze

½ cup (20 g) square cinnamon cereal

½ cup (120 ml) milk

1½ cups (180 g) confectioners' sugar

¼ tsp ground cinnamon

1 cup (40 g) square cinnamon cereal, for topping (optional)

DIRECTIONS

Preheat the oven to 350°F (180°C). Line two large baking sheets with parchment paper.

To make the cookies, place the cereal in a food processor or plastic bag. Process or crush the cereal into a fine, nut flour consistency. In a medium mixing bowl, whisk the finely crushed cereal, flour, cinnamon, baking soda, baking powder and salt until well combined. In the bowl of a stand mixer fitted with the paddle attachment, beat the butter and sugar on medium for 3 to 4 minutes, or until light and fluffy. Scrape the bottom and sides of the bowl as needed. Mix in the egg, egg yolk and vanilla, one at a time, until smooth and well combined. On low, mix the dry ingredients into the wet until just combined.

Scoop 2-tablespoon (30-g) amounts of the cookie dough onto the baking sheets, spacing them 2 inches (5 cm) apart. Bake for 9 to 11 minutes, or until the edges are set and lightly golden brown. Keep the cookies on the hot baking sheets for 5 minutes before transferring them to a cooling rack to cool to room temperature.

While the cookies cool, make the glaze. In a cereal bowl, add the cereal and pour the milk over it. Let the cereal sit in the milk for 20 minutes. Strain the cereal from the milk and discard (or eat!). In a medium mixing bowl, add the confectioners' sugar. Stir the cereal milk and cinnamon into the sugar until well combined. Drizzle the glaze on top of the cooled cookies. While the glaze is still wet, top the glaze with more cereal pieces if desired. Allow the glaze to set for 20 to 30 minutes before serving.

pumpkin snickerdoodle cookie sandwiches

makes 16 cookie sandwiches

These little pumpkin-filled cookies are full of fall flavor and deliciously irresistible textures. From the soft and fluffy pumpkin-spiced cookies with a spiced sugar coating to the sweet and tangy maple cream cheese frosting, these cookies are made for fall. Enjoy these cookies sandwiched together or alone with the buttercream and a dusting of cinnamon on top.

INGREDIENTS

for the pumpkin snickerdoodle cookies

2½ cups (300 g) all-purpose flour

2 tsp (6 g) pumpkin spice

2 tsp (5 g) cornstarch

1 tsp cream of tartar

½ tsp baking soda

½ tsp salt

¾ cup (170 g) unsalted butter, room temperature

¾ cup (150 g) granulated sugar

½ cup (100 g) light brown sugar

1 large egg yolk, room temperature

½ cup (125 g) pumpkin puree

2 tsp (10 ml) vanilla extract

for the spiced sugar

¼ cup (50 g) granulated sugar

1 tsp ground cinnamon

DIRECTIONS

To make the cookies, in a medium mixing bowl, whisk the flour, pumpkin spice, cornstarch, cream of tartar, baking soda and salt until well combined. In the bowl of a stand mixer fitted with the paddle attachment, beat the butter and sugars on medium for 3 to 4 minutes, or until light and fluffy. Scrape the bottom and sides of the bowl as needed.

On low, mix in the egg yolk, pumpkin puree and vanilla until smooth and well combined. On low, mix the dry ingredients into the wet until just combined. Cover the dough with plastic wrap, and chill it in the fridge for 60 minutes.

Preheat the oven to 375°F (190°C). Line two large baking sheets with parchment paper.

To make the spiced sugar, in a wide, shallow bowl, whisk the sugar and cinnamon until well combined. Set aside.

Scoop 1-tablespoon (15-g) amounts of chilled dough into your hands, roll them into balls and then roll the balls in the spiced sugar, coating them evenly. Place them onto the baking sheets, spacing them 2 inches (5 cm) apart. Bake for 10 to 12 minutes, or until the edges are set and lightly golden brown. Cool the cookies on the hot baking sheet for 3 to 4 minutes. Transfer to a cooling rack to cool completely to room temperature.

(continued)

pumpkin snickerdoodle cookie sandwiches (continued)

for the maple cream cheese buttercream

½ cup (113 g) unsalted butter, room temperature

4 oz (113 g) cream cheese, room temperature

2 tbsp (30 ml) maple syrup

1 tbsp (15 ml) milk

½ tsp ground cinnamon

½ tsp vanilla extract

¼ tsp salt

3 cups (360 g) confectioners' sugar

While the cookies cool, make the maple cream cheese buttercream. In the bowl of a stand mixer fitted with the paddle attachment, cream the butter and cream cheese for 3 to 4 minutes, or until creamy and well combined. Scrape the bottom and sides of the bowl as needed. On low, beat in the maple syrup, milk, cinnamon, vanilla and salt until smooth and well combined. On low, slowly add the confectioners' sugar, ½ cup (60 g) at a time. Once fully combined, taste and adjust the flavors as needed.

To assemble the cookie sandwiches, apply your desired amount of frosting to the bottom of one cookie. Place the bottom of another cookie to the frosted side of the first cookie and gently press together. Store cookies with frosting in an airtight container in the fridge.

parsnip thumbprints

makes 28 cookies

Although they are similar to carrots, parsnips may not be the first root vegetable you think of for baking, but they impart a wonderful spicy sweetness to anything they are baked into. With hints of licorice from the parsnips, these thumbprint cookies are sweet, spicy and a little unexpected. The honey cream cheese frosting complements and enhances the flavors of the soft, cake-like and spicy cookies it fills. If you're a fan of carrot cake, you will love these. Additionally, if parsnips are unavailable, carrots make an excellent replacement in this recipe.

INGREDIENTS

for the parsnip thumbprint cookies

1½ cups (180 g) all-purpose flour

½ cup (56 g) almond flour

1 tsp ground cinnamon

1 tsp ground ginger

½ tsp ground cloves

½ tsp salt

¾ cup (170 g) cubed unsalted butter, cold

½ cup (100 g) light brown sugar

¼ cup (50 g) granulated sugar

1 large egg yolk, room temperature

2 tsp (10 ml) vanilla extract

1 cup (100 g) finely shredded parsnips

1½ cups (168 g) finely chopped walnuts

DIRECTIONS

Line a large plate or small baking sheet with parchment or wax paper. This is just for chilling the cookie dough balls and will not be used for baking.

To make the cookies, in a medium mixing bowl, whisk together the all-purpose flour, almond flour, cinnamon, ginger, cloves and salt until well combined. In the bowl of a stand mixer fitted with the paddle attachment, beat the butter for 2 to 3 minutes, or until smooth. With the mixer on low, slowly add in the brown sugar and granulated sugar. Beat on medium-low speed until well combined. Increase the mixing speed to medium for 1 minute. Scrape the bottom and sides of the bowl as needed. With the mixer on low, mix in the egg yolk and vanilla. On low, mix the dry ingredients into the wet until just combined. Fold in the shredded parsnips until well combined. Place the walnuts in a bowl.

Scoop a 1-tablespoon (15-g) amount of cookie dough into your hands. Roll it into a smooth ball shape, then roll the ball in the chopped walnuts. Place the coated cookie dough ball onto the lined plate or baking sheet. Repeat for the remaining dough. Use a wine cork, your thumb or the back of a teaspoon to create an indentation in the center of each cookie. Place the cookie dough in the fridge to chill for 30 to 60 minutes, or until solid.

Preheat the oven to 350°F (180°C). Line a large baking sheet with parchment paper.

Place each of the dough balls on the baking sheet, spacing them 2 inches (5 cm) apart. Bake the cookies for 12 to 14 minutes, or until the edges of the cookies are set and a light golden brown color. Cool the cookies on the pan for 5 minutes. While they are still warm, use your thumb or the teaspoon to remake the indentation. Transfer the cookies to a cooling rack to cool to room temperature.

(continued)

for the honey cream cheese frosting

¼ cup (57 g) unsalted butter, room temperature

4 oz (113 g) cream cheese, room temperature

1–2 tsp (5–10 ml) honey

1 tsp vanilla extract

¼ tsp salt

1½ cups (180 g) confectioners' sugar

While the cookies cool, make the honey cream cheese frosting. In the bowl of a stand mixer fitted with the paddle attachment, cream the butter and cream cheese for 3 to 4 minutes, or until creamy and well combined. Scrape the bottom and sides of the bowl as needed. On low, beat in the honey, vanilla and salt until smooth and well combined. On low, mix in the confectioners' sugar slowly, ½ cup (60 g) at a time. Once fully combined, taste and adjust the flavors as needed.

Once the cookies are completely cooled to room temperature, fill each indentation with 1 to 1½ teaspoons (5 to 8 ml) of honey cream cheese frosting. These cookies should be stored in an airtight container in the fridge.

churro cookies

makes 22 cookies

Churros are one of my favorite desserts. There is something so deliciously irresistible about the contrast of soft, fried dough with a crunchy cinnamon-sugar coating. Dip them into a chocolate or caramel sauce and it's just perfection. These are my take on this most beloved Mexican dessert. Once coated in a sweet glaze and spiced sugar, these churro cookies look and taste just like their namesake dessert.

INGREDIENTS

for the churro cookies

2¾ cups (330 g) all-purpose flour

2 tsp (6 g) ground cinnamon

½ tsp baking powder

¼ tsp salt

1 cup (226 g) unsalted butter, room temperature

1 cup (200 g) granulated sugar

1 egg, room temperature

2 tsp (10 ml) vanilla extract

¼ tsp almond extract (optional)

for the spiced sugar and glaze

½ cup (120 ml) water

½ cup (60 g) confectioners' sugar

½ cup (100 g) granulated sugar

1½ tsp (7 g) ground cinnamon

¼ tsp chili powder (optional)

for the chocolate ganache

4 oz (113 g) semisweet or bittersweet chocolate, evenly chopped

½ cup (120 ml) heavy cream

¼ tsp vanilla extract

special baking supplies

Piping bag

Atteco #828 piping tip

DIRECTIONS

Preheat the oven to 375°F (190°C). Line two large baking sheets with parchment paper.

To make the cookies, in a medium mixing bowl, whisk together the flour, cinnamon, baking powder and salt until well combined. In the bowl of a stand mixer fitted with the paddle attachment, beat the butter and sugar on medium, for 3 to 4 minutes, or until light, fluffy and well combined. Scrape the bottom and sides of the bowl as needed. On low, beat in the egg, vanilla and almond extract (if using) until smooth and well combined. On low, mix the dry ingredients into the wet until just combined.

Transfer half of the dough into a large piping bag fitted with a wide star attachment (Atteco #828). Pipe 3- to 4-inch (8- to 10-cm)-long cookies onto the baking sheets, spacing them 1 inch (2.5 cm) apart. Bake for 12 to 16 minutes, or until the edges are set and lightly golden brown. While the first batch of cookies bakes, pipe the remaining dough onto the second baking sheet. If your kitchen is particularly warm, place the piped unbaked cookies in the fridge while the first batch bakes. Keep the cookies on the hot baking sheet for 3 to 4 minutes before transferring them to a cooling rack to cool completely.

While the cookies cool, make the spiced sugar and glaze. In a wide, shallow bowl, whisk together the water and confectioners' sugar until well combined. In another wide, shallow bowl, whisk together the granulated sugar, cinnamon and chili powder (if using) until very well combined. Taste and adjust the spices as needed. This glaze is meant to be very thin. Quickly dip the cookies in the glaze. Shake off any excess liquid. Roll in the spiced sugar. Place the coated cookies back onto the cooling rack to set.

To make the ganache, place the chocolate in a wide, shallow bowl. Heat the heavy cream in a saucepan (or use the microwave) until just scalding. Pour the steaming cream on top of the chocolate. Let it sit for 3 minutes. Add the vanilla and whisk until smooth and well combined. Dip the churros into the chocolate ganache and enjoy!

maple-frosted sour cream

makes 28 cookies

These no-chill cookies are like a cross between a cookie and a muffin top.
They are lightly spiced, allowing the flavors of the maple frosting to shine through.
Think of these as the deliciously soft and fluffy bites of fall.

INGREDIENTS

for the brown butter
½ cup + 2 tbsp (141 g) unsalted butter

for the spiced sour cream cookies
1¼ cups (150 g) all-purpose flour

1 tsp apple pie spice or pumpkin spice

½ tsp baking powder

⅛ tsp baking soda

¼ tsp salt

¼ cup (57 g) unsalted butter, room temperature

½ cup (100 g) granulated sugar

¼ cup (50 g) light brown sugar

1 large egg, room temperature

1 tsp vanilla extract

½ cup (120 ml) sour cream, room temperature

for the maple frosting
Prepared brown butter from above

1½ cups (180 g) confectioners' sugar, divided

1–2 tbsp (15–30 ml) maple syrup

1 tsp vanilla extract

1 tbsp (15 ml) milk, plus more as needed

DIRECTIONS

To make the brown butter, melt the butter in a heavy bottom saucepan over medium heat for 7 to 10 minutes, or until the butter starts to foam. Whisk continuously until brown bits start to form. Depending on your stove and saucepan, the entire process should take 10 to 15 minutes. Immediately remove the pan from the heat, and pour the brown butter into a clean bowl to cool for 30 minutes, or until it reaches room temperature. Transfer the bowl to the fridge to solidify for 1½ to 2 hours, or until the butter reaches a softened texture.

Preheat the oven to 375°F (190°C). Line two large baking sheets with parchment paper.

To make the cookies, in a medium mixing bowl, whisk together the flour, apple pie spice, baking powder, baking soda and salt until well combined. In the bowl of a stand mixer fitted with the paddle attachment, beat the butter and sugars on medium speed for 3 to 4 minutes, or until light and fluffy. Scrape the bottom and sides of the bowl as needed. Mix in the egg, vanilla and sour cream until smooth and well combined. On low, mix the dry ingredients into the wet until just combined.

Scoop 1-tablespoon (15-g) amounts of cookie dough onto the baking sheets, spacing them 2 inches (5 cm) apart. Bake for 9 to 11 minutes, or until the edges are set and a finger pressed gently into the center of the cookie bounces back. The cookies will still look lighter in color. Keep the cookies on the hot baking sheet for 3 to 4 minutes before transferring them to a cooling rack to cool completely.

While the cookies cool, make the maple frosting. In the bowl of a stand mixer fitted with the paddle attachment, cream the prepared brown butter and 1 cup (120 g) of the confectioners' sugar for 3 to 4 minutes, or until smooth and well combined. Scrape the bottom and sides of the bowl as needed. On low, beat in the maple syrup, vanilla, milk and remaining confectioners' sugar until smooth and well combined. Spread the frosting on top of the cooled cookies. Store the frosted cookies in an airtight container in the fridge and unfrosted cookies in an airtight container at room temperature.

gingerbread cookie bars

makes 1 (8 x 8" [20 x 20–cm]) pan

One of my absolute favorite baked goods is gingerbread. I could eat it all year long. For these cookies, I wanted a cookie bar that was reminiscent of gingerbread with the texture of a chewy shortbread. This recipe transforms the scents and flavors you know and love from gingerbread into a soft and buttery shortbread-esque cookie bar. These are topped with a sweetened cream cheese glaze that perfectly balances the dark, sweet and spicy flavors of the cookie base.

INGREDIENTS

for the gingerbread cookie bars

2 cups (240 g) all-purpose flour

¼ cup (28 g) almond flour

1 tsp ground cinnamon

1 tsp ground ginger

½ tsp ground cloves or allspice

¼ tsp ground nutmeg

¼ tsp salt

1 cup (200 g) light brown sugar

Zest of 1 lemon

1 cup (226 g) unsalted butter, room temperature

1 large egg yolk, room temperature

2 tbsp (30 ml) molasses

for the cream cheese glaze

2 oz (57 g) cream cheese, room temperature

1 tbsp (15 ml) milk, plus more as needed

½ tsp vanilla extract

1 cup (120 g) confectioners' sugar

DIRECTIONS

Preheat the oven to 350°F (180°C). Line an 8 x 8–inch (20 x 20–cm) metal pan with parchment paper, leaving an overhang of 1 to 2 inches (2.5 to 5 cm) on two sides to allow for easy removal.

To make the cookie bars, in a medium mixing bowl, whisk together the all-purpose flour, almond flour, cinnamon, ginger, cloves, nutmeg and salt. In the bowl of a stand mixer fitted with the paddle attachment, add the brown sugar and zest. On low speed, mix the sugar and zest until the texture resembles wet sand. Add the butter, and on medium speed, beat the butter and lemon sugar for 3 to 4 minutes, or until light and fluffy. Scrape the bottom and sides of the bowl as needed. Mix in the egg yolk and molasses until smooth and well combined. On low speed, mix the dry ingredients into the wet until just combined. If needed, use a spatula or your hands to work any stray pieces into the dough. Evenly press the dough into the prepared pan. Bake for 25 to 35 minutes, or until the edges are set and pull away slightly from the edge of the pan. Cool the cookie in the pan for 10 minutes.

While the cookie cools, make the glaze. In a medium mixing bowl, add the cream cheese. Stir in the milk and vanilla until well combined. Stir in the confectioners' sugar until well combined. If needed, add up to 1 tablespoon (15 ml) of additional milk until the glaze is pourable. Pour the glaze on top of the cookie bars inside the pan. Once the glaze is set, cut the bars into your preferred size. Transfer the bars from the pan to the cooling rack to finish cooling and setting. Glazed cookie bars should be stored in an airtight container in the fridge.

apple cider sugar

makes 32 cookies

These soft cookies are full of fresh, tart apple cider flavor, which is balanced with lots of warming spices, butter and sugar. The texture is similar to the classic sugar cookie you know and love, just with a unique apple cider twist. In other words, these cookies are a fantastic way to put your fresh apple cider to good use.

INGREDIENTS

for the apple cider sugar cookies

2 cups (480 ml) apple cider

2½ cups (300 g) all-purpose flour

2 tsp (6 g) apple pie spice

2 tsp (9 g) baking powder

2 tsp (5 g) cornstarch

½ tsp salt

¾ cup (170 g) unsalted butter, room temperature

1 cup (200 g) granulated sugar

¼ cup (50 g) light brown sugar

1 large egg, room temperature

1 large egg yolk, room temperature

2 tsp (10 ml) vanilla extract

for the spiced sugar

¼ cup (50 g) granulated sugar

1 tsp apple pie spice or ground cinnamon

DIRECTIONS

To make the cookies, add the apple cider to a medium skillet. Over medium-high heat, bring it to a boil for 12 to 15 minutes, or until the cider reduces down to ¼ cup (60 ml) and is thick like a syrup. Pour this into a heat-safe bowl or cup and cool to room temperature. In a separate bowl, whisk together the flour, apple pie spice, baking powder, cornstarch and salt until well combined. In the bowl of a stand mixer fitted with the paddle attachment, cream the butter and sugars together on medium speed for 3 to 4 minutes, or until light and fluffy. With the mixer on low, beat in, one at a time, the reduced apple cider, egg, egg yolk and vanilla. Scrape the bottom and sides of the bowl as needed. Mix on low for 1 minute. With the mixer on low, mix the dry ingredients into the wet until just combined. Cover the dough with plastic wrap and chill for 30 to 60 minutes. The dough is ready when it can easily hold its shape when scooped.

Make the spiced sugar by whisking together the sugar and apple pie spice or ground cinnamon in a wide, shallow bowl until well combined.

Preheat the oven to 375°F (190°C). Line two baking sheets with parchment paper.

Scoop 1-tablespoon (15-g) amounts of the cookie dough into your hands, roll the dough into balls and roll the balls in the spiced sugar, coating them evenly. Place the cookie dough balls onto the baking sheets, spacing them 2 inches (5 cm) apart. Bake for 10 to 12 minutes, or until the edges are set and lightly golden brown. Keep the cookies on the hot baking sheets for 3 to 4 minutes before transferring them to a cooling rack to cool to room temperature.

chai hazelnut blondie bars

makes 1 (8 x 8" [20 x 20-cm]) pan

I absolutely love baking with a blend of all-purpose and nut flours. Nut flours bring a chewy texture and nutty flavor that I find incredibly delicious. These bars use hazelnut flour and a blend of chai spices to bring a spicy, warm and nutty twist to these classic cookie bars. Top these with a maple buttercream and hazelnuts for a truly decadent cookie bar.

INGREDIENTS

for the chai hazelnut blondie bars

1½ cups (180 g) all-purpose flour

½ cup (56 g) hazelnut flour (see tip)

½ tsp salt

½ tsp ground cinnamon

½ tsp ground cardamom

½ tsp ground ginger

¼ tsp ground cloves

¼ tsp ground nutmeg

¼ tsp baking powder

½ cup + 2 tbsp (141 g) unsalted butter

¾ cup (150 g) light brown sugar

1 egg, room temperature

1 egg yolk, room temperature

2 tsp (10 ml) vanilla extract

for the maple buttercream

½ cup (113 g) unsalted butter, room temperature

2 cups (250 g) sifted confectioners' sugar

2 tbsp (30 ml) pure maple syrup

½ tsp vanilla extract

¼ tsp salt

1 tbsp (15 ml) milk, plus more as needed

½ cup (56 g) roughly chopped hazelnuts

DIRECTIONS

Preheat the oven to 350°F (180°C). Line an 8 x 8–inch (20 x 20–cm) metal pan with parchment paper, leaving an overhang of 1 to 2 inches (2.5 to 5 cm) on two sides to allow for easy removal.

To make the bars, in a medium mixing bowl, whisk together the flour, hazelnut flour, salt, cinnamon, cardamom, ginger, cloves, nutmeg and baking powder. Melt the butter in a heavy bottom saucepan over medium heat for 7 to 10 minutes, or until the butter starts to foam. Whisk continuously until brown bits start to form. Immediately remove the pan from the heat, and pour the brown butter into a clean bowl to cool slightly. Whisk in the brown sugar until smooth and well combined. Whisk in the egg, egg yolk and vanilla until smooth and well combined. Stir the dry ingredients into the wet until just combined. Evenly spread the cookie batter across the prepared pan. Bake for 30 to 35 minutes, or until the blondies are golden brown with the edges pulling away slightly from the pan. Cool the blondies in the pan on top of a cooling rack for 20 to 30 minutes, or until they have cooled completely to room temperature.

While the blondies cool, make the buttercream. In the bowl of a stand mixer fitted with the paddle attachment, cream the butter until smooth. On low, mix in the confectioners' sugar, ½ cup (60 g) at a time. Once all the sugar has been added, mix in the maple syrup, vanilla, salt and milk. Mix the buttercream on low until all the ingredients are smooth and well combined. If the buttercream is too thick, add up to 2 tablespoons (30 ml) of additional milk. Spread the maple buttercream on top of the cooled blondie bars. Top with the chopped hazelnuts, slice and enjoy.

tip: To make homemade hazelnut flour, grind ½ cup (56 to 66 g) of hazelnuts in a food processor to the consistency of almond flour. You could also use almond flour as a substitute for the hazelnut flour. In that case, top with sliced almonds instead of hazelnuts.

ginger s'mores cookies

makes 22 cookies

These molasses-filled, marshmallow-topped cookies are inspired by the classic campfire treat. Although I believe s'mores season is year-round, I really wanted to create a cookie that fits in perfectly with the colder seasons of the year. These cookies balance the spicy, dark flavors of ginger and molasses with pools of sweet milk chocolate and lightly toasted marshmallow crème. They are the nostalgic campfire treat with a sweet and spicy twist!

INGREDIENTS

2¼ cups (270 g) all-purpose flour

2 tsp (4 g) ground ginger

1 tsp ground cinnamon

1½ tsp (7 g) baking soda

½ tsp salt

¾ cup (170 g) unsalted butter, room temperature

¾ cup (150 g) granulated sugar

½ cup (100 g) light brown sugar

¼ cup (60 ml) molasses

1 large egg, room temperature

2 tsp (10 ml) vanilla extract

1 tsp freshly grated ginger

9 oz (255 g) milk chocolate, roughly chopped

7 oz (198 g) marshmallow crème

DIRECTIONS

In a medium mixing bowl, whisk together the flour, ground ginger, cinnamon, baking soda and salt. Set aside. In the bowl of a stand mixer fitted with the paddle attachment, cream the butter and sugars together on medium speed for 3 minutes, or until well combined. With the mixer on low, stream in the molasses. Once the molasses is fully added, turn up the mixer speed to medium, and cream for 1 minute or until fully combined. Scrape the bottom and sides of the bowl as needed. On low, beat in the egg, vanilla and fresh ginger until fully combined. Mix the dry ingredients into the wet until just combined. Mix in the milk chocolate until combined. Wrap the dough in plastic wrap, and chill it in the fridge for at least 2 hours and up to overnight.

Preheat the oven to 350°F (180°C). Line a large baking sheet with parchment paper. Let the dough sit out at room temperature for 30 minutes before baking.

Scoop 2-tablespoon (30-g) amounts of cookie dough onto the baking sheet, spacing them 3 inches (8 cm) apart. The cookies will spread while baking. Using a teaspoon-sized (5-g) measuring spoon, top each cookie dough ball with marshmallow crème. Dip the teaspoon into a glass of hot water as needed. This helps the marshmallow crème scoop more easily. Bake for 12 to 14 minutes, or until the edges of the cookies are set. Both the cookies and the crème topping will spread while the cookies bake. Some of the crème may melt slightly, but most should bake on top of the cookie. Keep the cookies on the hot baking sheet for 5 minutes before transferring them to a cooling rack to cool to room temperature.

spiced wine crinkle

makes 24 cookies

These cookies are inspired by one of the coziest winter drinks: mulled wine. I wanted to capture the scents and flavors of mulled wine, while also creating a cookie that could be enjoyed with or without a glass of wine. The end result is a crinkle cookie with all the wonderfully delicious and complex aromas of spiced wine baked in. Next time you make some mulled wine, be sure to make a batch of these cookies as well! If you don't have mulled wine in your plans, these cookies are still delicious with your favorite red wine or orange juice instead.

INGREDIENTS

for the spiced wine crinkle cookies

2 cups (240 g) all-purpose flour

1½ tsp (7 g) baking powder

2 tsp (6 g) ground cinnamon

½ tsp ground cardamom

½ tsp ground cloves

½ tsp ground nutmeg

¼ tsp salt

1 cup (200 g) granulated sugar

Zest of 1 medium orange

5 tbsp (75 ml) melted unsalted butter

1 tsp vanilla extract

2 large eggs, room temperature

2 tbsp (30 ml) mulled wine, red wine or orange juice

for the spiced sugar

¼ cup (50 g) granulated sugar

1 tsp ground cinnamon

½ cup (60 g) confectioners' sugar

DIRECTIONS

To make the cookies, in a medium mixing bowl, whisk together the flour, baking powder, cinnamon, cardamom, cloves, nutmeg and salt until well combined. Add the sugar and zest to a large mixing bowl, and whisk until the sugar starts to feel like wet sand. Whisk in the melted butter and vanilla until smooth and well combined. Whisk in the eggs and wine until smooth and well combined. Stir the dry ingredients into the wet until well combined. Cover the dough with plastic wrap. Chill it in the fridge for at least 2 hours and up to 2 days.

Make the spiced sugar by whisking together the granulated sugar and cinnamon in a wide, shallow bowl until well combined. Pour the confectioners' sugar into another wide, shallow bowl.

Preheat the oven to 350°F (180°C). Line two baking sheets with parchment paper.

Scoop 1 tablespoon (15 g) of cookie dough into your hands. Roll it into a ball, then roll the ball in the spiced sugar, making sure to fully coat it. Roll the sugar-covered ball in the confectioners' sugar, making sure to fully coat it. Place the covered dough ball onto a baking sheet. Repeat with the remaining dough, leaving 2 inches (5 cm) of space between each cookie. Bake the cookies for 10 to 12 minutes, or until the edges of the cookies are set, the centers are raised and the cookies look cracked. Keep the cookies on the hot baking sheets for 5 minutes before transferring them to a cooling rack to cool completely.

salted caramel gingerbread skillet cookie

makes 1 (9" [23-cm]) skillet cookie

Sweet and salty caramel is the perfect complement to this dark, spicy gingerbread cookie. Because this cookie is baked in a skillet, the edges are crisp, while the center stays gooey. I highly recommend serving this with vanilla ice cream and more salted caramel. For a quick and easy version, this recipe is just as delicious with a store-bought caramel sauce.

INGREDIENTS

for the caramel filling
1 cup (200 g) granulated sugar
6 tbsp (85 g) unsalted butter
⅔ cup (160 ml) heavy cream
½ tsp salt

for the gingerbread cookie
1¾ cups (210 g) all-purpose flour
½ tsp baking soda
½ tsp baking powder
1½ tsp (3 g) ground ginger
1 tsp ground cinnamon
½ tsp ground cloves
¼ tsp ground nutmeg
¼ tsp salt
½ cup (113 g) unsalted butter, room temperature
1¼ cups (250 g) light brown sugar
2 tbsp (30 ml) molasses
2 large eggs, room temperature
1 tsp vanilla extract

Vanilla ice cream, for serving

tip: Make the caramel ahead of time. Store it in the fridge and bring it to room temperature before using.

DIRECTIONS

To make the caramel filling, heat the sugar in a medium saucepan over medium-low heat. Once the sugar begins to melt, stir continuously until fully melted. Whisk in the butter. Once the butter has fully melted, cook for 1 minute without stirring. Slowly stir in the heavy cream. Once all the cream has been added and the mixture bubbles up in the pan, remove the pan from the heat. Stir in the salt until fully incorporated. Pour the hot caramel sauce into a heatproof container to cool to room temperature.

Preheat the oven to 350°F (180°C). Lightly grease a cast-iron skillet.

To make the skillet cookie, in a medium mixing bowl, whisk together the flour, baking soda, baking powder, ground ginger, cinnamon, cloves, nutmeg and salt until well combined. In the bowl of a stand mixer fitted with the paddle attachment, cream the butter and sugar on medium speed for 3 minutes, or until well combined. With the mixer on low, stream in the molasses. Turn up the mixer speed to medium, and cream for 1 minute, or until fully combined. Scrape the bottom and sides of the bowl as needed. On low, beat in the eggs and vanilla until fully combined. With the mixer on low, mix the dry ingredients into the wet until combined. Evenly spread the cookie dough into the prepared skillet. Drop tablespoon-sized (15-ml) drops of caramel sauce into the cookie dough. This skillet cookie works well with ¼ to ½ cup (60 to 120 ml) of caramel sauce. Reserve the remaining sauce for topping and serving.

Bake the cookie for 35 to 40 minutes, or until the edges of the cookie are set and pull slightly from the edge of the skillet. The center may still look slightly underbaked, but don't worry as the cookie will continue to "bake" from the residual heat while cooling. Cool the cookie in the skillet placed on a cooling rack for 30 minutes, or until the pan is cool enough to touch. Top with additional caramel sauce and vanilla ice cream right before serving.

Chocolate

roasted sweetness

Chocolate is an ingredient so synonymous with flavor that it could practically be called a spice. From rich, dark and barely sweetened, to milky sweet with notes of caramel, chocolate is as nuanced in flavor as any other spice. The title of this chapter is a nod to the method in which the cocoa bean is prepared and processed into this beloved and iconic ingredient.

In this chapter you will find more blends of spices than in other chapters. Chocolate has a way of overpowering the other flavors that can often fall flat rather than standing out. Spice blends such as chai in the Brown Butter Kitchen Sink cookies (page 70) and the pumpkin in the Chocolate Pumpkin Crinkle cookies (page 69) allow those spices to balance, enhance and shine alongside the chocolate. You'll also find espresso powder is used in many of the recipes. This is because chocolate and espresso share very similar flavor profiles. When espresso powder is paired with chocolate, it brings out more of the richer, darker, more chocolaty notes. In other words, it makes the chocolate taste more like chocolate!

tahini chocolate chip

makes 16 cookies

Tahini is a Middle Eastern condiment made from toasted, ground hulled sesame. It is often used in savory recipes such as hummus. However, when it's used in baking, tahini brings a lovely earthy and nutty flavor that complements and even tames the sweetness of baked goods. These cookies are just like the iconic ones you know and love with an earthy, nutty and slightly savory flavor.

INGREDIENTS

2¼ cups (270 g) all-purpose flour

2 tsp (5 g) cornstarch

2 tsp (6 g) ground cinnamon

½ tsp baking soda

1 tsp salt

¾ cup (170 g) unsalted butter, room temperature

1 cup (200 g) light brown sugar

¼ cup (50 g) granulated sugar

¼ cup (57 g) tahini, well stirred (see tips)

1 large egg, room temperature

1 large egg yolk, room temperature

2 tsp (10 ml) vanilla extract

12 oz (340 g) semisweet, milk chocolate or dark chocolate, chopped into chunks, divided

Flaky salt, for topping (optional)

DIRECTIONS

In a medium mixing bowl, whisk together the flour, cornstarch, cinnamon, baking soda and salt until well combined. In the bowl of a stand mixer fitted with the paddle attachment, cream the butter and sugars on medium speed for 3 minutes, or until light and fluffy. On medium speed, beat in the tahini for 1 to 2 minutes, or until very well combined. Beat in, one at a time for 20 seconds, the egg, egg yolk and vanilla on low. Scrape the bottom and sides of the bowl as needed. With the mixer on low, add the dry ingredients into the wet until just combined. Scrape the bottom and sides of the bowl as needed.

Fold in 9 ounces (255 g) of the chopped chocolate until combined. Cover the cookie dough and chill it in the fridge for at least 1 hour and up to overnight. The longer the dough chills, the chewier the texture and more developed the flavor will be.

Preheat the oven to 350°F (180°C). Line two large baking sheets with parchment paper. Allow the cookie dough to sit out at room temperature for 20 to 30 minutes before baking.

Scoop 2-tablespoon (30-g) amounts of cookie dough balls onto the baking sheets, spacing them 3 inches (8 cm) apart. Top the balls with the remaining chocolate chunks. Bake for 10 to 12 minutes, or until the edges are golden brown and the centers are just baked through. Keep the cookies on the hot baking sheets for 5 minutes before transferring them to a cooling rack to cool to room temperature. Top with flaky salt, if desired.

tips: While the cookies are still hot from the oven, use a large biscuit or cookie cutter that's wider than the cookies to help shape any cookies into a rounder shape. If you prefer to substitute the tahini, use the same amount of cashew or almond butter.

tiramisu brownie cookies

makes 10 cookie sandwiches

Tiramisu is a classic Italian dessert made from espresso and liqueur-soaked ladyfingers, layered with a sweetened mascarpone-based filling and topped with a dusting of cocoa powder. Tiramisu also happens to be my favorite dessert, so I knew early on that I wanted to have a tiramisu-inspired cookie in this book. This recipe replaces the ladyfingers with fudge-like, crackle-topped brownie cookies and sandwiches them together with a creamy, sweetened espresso mascarpone filling.

INGREDIENTS

for the espresso mascarpone filling

2 tbsp (18 g) instant espresso powder

2 tbsp (30 ml) warm water

8 oz (226 g) mascarpone cheese, room temperature

1 tsp vanilla bean paste or vanilla extract

¼ tsp salt

2 cups (240 g) confectioners' sugar

for the tiramisu brownie cookies

½ cup (113 g) cubed unsalted butter

8 oz (226 g) good-quality dark (70% or higher cocoa content) chocolate bar, chopped

1 cup (200 g) granulated sugar

2 large eggs, room temperature

¼ cup (24 g) Dutch process cocoa powder

2 tsp (6 g) instant espresso powder

2 tsp (6 g) ground cinnamon

1 tsp baking powder

½ tsp salt

¾ cup (90 g) all-purpose flour

DIRECTIONS

To make the filling, in a medium mixing bowl, mix the espresso powder with the warm water. Set aside to cool to room temperature. Add the mascarpone to the bowl of a stand mixer fitted with the paddle attachment. On the lowest speed, spread the mascarpone cheese across the bottom of the bowl. This should take only a few rotations. Add 1 tablespoon (15 ml) of the brewed espresso, the vanilla bean paste and salt. Mix on the lowest speed until smooth and well combined. Sift in the confectioners' sugar. Mix on low until smooth and well combined. If the filling is too thick, add more brewed espresso, 1 teaspoon at a time and up to 3 teaspoons (15 ml) total, until the texture is to your liking. Pour into an airtight container and store in the fridge until you are ready to assemble the cookies.

Preheat the oven to 350°F (180°C). Line two large baking sheets with parchment paper.

To make the cookies, place the butter and chopped chocolate in a microwave-safe bowl, and heat in the microwave for 1 minute. Carefully pull out the bowl. Stir the melted butter and partially melted chocolate until they are well combined. Heat in 20-second increments, stirring until the butter and chocolate are fully melted and well combined.

(continued)

In the bowl of a stand mixer fitted with the whisk attachment, whisk the sugar and eggs on medium speed for 4 to 5 minutes, or until light, fluffy and pale yellow. On low, slowly stream in the melted chocolate mixture. Beat the mixture until well combined. Scrape the bottom and sides of the bowl as needed. Sift in the cocoa powder, espresso powder, cinnamon, baking powder and salt. Whisk on low until smooth and well combined. Scrape the bottom and sides of the bowl as needed. Sift in the flour. Whisk on low until the flour is fully combined. Scrape the bottom and sides of the bowl as needed. Whisk on low for 20 to 30 seconds to fully incorporate any stray pieces of flour.

Scoop 2-tablespoon (30-g) amounts of the brownie cookie dough onto the baking sheets, spacing them 2 inches (5 cm) apart. Try to scoop all the brownie cookie batter onto the baking sheets to bake at the same time. Bake on the center rack for 10 to 11 minutes, or until the edges are fully set. The centers will be cracked and barely set. Cool the cookies on the baking sheet placed on top of a cooling rack until fully cooled.

To assemble, apply the desired amount of filling to the bottom of one cookie. Place the bottom of another cookie to the filling side of the first cookie. Gently press together and enjoy!

chai chocolate chip cookie cake

makes 1 (9" [23-cm]) cookie cake

Growing up, I would always ask for a giant cookie cake to celebrate my birthday. There was something so exciting about going to the mall and selecting the design I wanted piped onto the giant cookie. Not to mention actually getting to cut into and enjoy the cake! The middle part will forever be my favorite. This cookie cake is my grown-up version of my favorite childhood celebratory treat. The tahini buttercream pairs beautifully with the chai spice blend and chocolate chip cookie. Feel free to use regular buttercream if you like, but don't forget the sprinkles!

INGREDIENTS

for the chocolate chip cookie cake

1¾ cups (210 g) all-purpose flour

1 tbsp (10 g) cornstarch

1 tsp ground cinnamon

1 tsp ground ginger

1 tsp ground cardamom

½ tsp ground cloves

½ tsp ground nutmeg

½ tsp baking powder

½ tsp baking soda

½ tsp salt

½ cup (120 ml) melted unsalted butter

½ cup (100 g) light brown sugar

½ cup (100 g) granulated sugar

1 large egg, room temperature

1 tsp vanilla extract

1 cup (170 g) semisweet or milk chocolate chips, divided

DIRECTIONS

Preheat the oven to 350°F (180°C). Lightly grease the bottom of a 9-inch (23-cm) springform pan, and line it with parchment paper.

To make the cake, in a medium mixing bowl, whisk together the flour, cornstarch, cinnamon, ginger, cardamom, cloves, nutmeg, baking powder, baking soda and salt. In a large mixing bowl, whisk together the butter, sugars, egg and vanilla until smooth and well combined. Stir the dry ingredients into the wet until just combined. Fold in ¾ cup (130 g) of the chocolate chips. Evenly spread the cookie dough into the prepared pan. Top with the remaining chocolate chips. Bake for 25 to 30 minutes, or until the edges of the cookie are set and pull slightly from the edge of the skillet. Cool the cookie in the pan placed on a cooling rack for 30 minutes or until the pan is cool enough to touch. Run a butter knife around the edges of the pan to loosen any cookie that may be stuck to the pan. Remove the springform pan ring. Allow the cookie cake to cool completely to room temperature.

(continued)

chai chocolate chip cookie cake (continued)

for the tahini buttercream

½ cup (113 g) unsalted butter, room temperature

¼ cup (57 g) tahini, well stirred (see tip)

1½ cups (180 g) confectioners' sugar, divided

1 tsp vanilla extract

¼ tsp salt

1–2 tbsp (15–30 ml) milk (optional)

Sprinkles or chocolate shavings, for topping

While the cookie cools, make the tahini buttercream. In the bowl of a stand mixer fitted with the paddle attachment, cream the butter and tahini for 4 to 5 minutes, or until creamy and well combined. Scrape the bottom and sides of the bowl as needed. On low, beat in ½ cup (60 g) of the confectioners' sugar, vanilla and salt until smooth and well combined. Scrape down the bottom and sides of the bowl as needed. On medium speed, beat in the remaining confectioners' sugar, and then beat on medium speed until the frosting reaches your desired consistency. If the frosting is too thick, mix in 1 to 2 tablespoons (15 to 30 ml) of milk. Transfer the buttercream to a pastry bag fitted with your desired piping tip.

To assemble, slide the cooled chocolate chip cookie cake to a serving plate. Pipe frosting around the edges of the cookie. Top the piped frosting with sprinkles or chocolate shavings for a celebratory touch.

tip: For a more traditional buttercream, replace the tahini with ¼ cup (57 g) of room-temperature unsalted butter.

bourbon toffee chocolate chip

makes 12 cookies

These cookies are buttery, sweet, salty and filled with melted pieces of sweet milk chocolate and toffee. The bourbon both complements and balances the sweet and salty parts of the cookie. In short, these are everything you could want in a cookie and more.

INGREDIENTS

1¾ cups (210 g) all-purpose flour

2 tbsp (20 g) cornstarch

2 tsp (6 g) ground cinnamon

½ tsp baking powder

½ tsp baking soda

¼ tsp salt

½ cup (113 g) cubed unsalted butter, cold

½ cup (100 g) light brown sugar

¼ cup (50 g) granulated sugar

1 large egg, room temperature

1 tsp vanilla extract

1 tbsp (15 ml) bourbon whiskey

½ cup (90 g) chopped toffee pieces

1 cup (170 g) milk chocolate chips

Flaky salt, for topping

DIRECTIONS

Preheat the oven to 375°F (190°C). Line two large baking sheets with parchment paper.

In a medium mixing bowl, whisk together the flour, cornstarch, cinnamon, baking powder, baking soda and salt until well combined. In the bowl of a stand mixer fitted with the paddle attachment, beat the butter on medium-high speed for 2 minutes. Scrape the bottom and sides of the bowl as needed. Beat the sugars into the butter on low speed. Once all the sugar has been added, beat on medium speed for 3 minutes, or until light, fluffy and well combined. Scrape the bottom and sides of the bowl as needed. On low, beat in the egg, vanilla and bourbon whiskey until smooth and well combined. With the mixer on low, mix the dry ingredients into the wet until just combined. Fold in the toffee pieces and chocolate chips.

Scoop 3-tablespoon (45-g) amounts of the dough; you should have 12 equally sized pieces. Form each of the pieces of cookie dough into a ball. Place six cookie dough balls onto each baking sheet.

Bake for 9 to 12 minutes, or until the cookies have lightly golden and set edges. The cookies will be very fragrant. While the cookies are still warm, top with the flaky salt. Cool cookies on the hot baking sheet until completely cooled to room temperature.

nutella®-filled chocolate sugar cookies

makes 14–16 cookies

Although these cookies may look like any other chocolate sugar cookie, they are most definitely not. From soft and chewy, to crunchy and creamy, these cookies have layers of contrasting textures that makes them utterly irresistible. The sweet aroma of chai spices pairs beautifully with the chocolate cookie, while the creamy chocolate-hazelnut filling makes these cookies delightfully indulgent.

INGREDIENTS

for the nutella-filled
chocolate sugar cookies

1 cup (320 g) chocolate-hazelnut spread (I prefer Nutella brand)

2 cups (240 g) all-purpose flour

2 tsp (9 g) baking powder

½ tsp ground cinnamon

½ tsp ground cardamom

½ tsp ground ginger

¼ tsp ground cloves

¼ tsp ground nutmeg

½ tsp salt

1 cup (226 g) unsalted butter, room temperature

1 cup (200 g) granulated sugar

¼ cup (50 g) light brown sugar

½ cup (48 g) Dutch process cocoa powder

2 large eggs, room temperature

for the cinnamon sugar

¼ cup (50 g) granulated sugar

1 tsp ground cinnamon

DIRECTIONS

Line a large plate or baking sheet with wax paper.

To make the cookies, scoop out 16 (1-tablespoon [15-g]-sized) dollops of Nutella. Place them on the wax paper–lined plate or baking sheet and place it in the freezer. In a medium mixing bowl, whisk together the flour, baking powder, cinnamon, cardamom, ginger, cloves, nutmeg and salt until well combined. In the bowl of a stand mixer fitted with the paddle attachment, cream the butter and sugars on medium speed for 3 minutes, or until well combined. On low, mix in the cocoa powder until smooth and well combined. Scrape the bottom and sides of the bowl as needed. Mix in the eggs until smooth and well combined. Scrape the bottom and sides of the bowl as needed. On low, mix the dry ingredients into the wet until just combined. Wrap the dough in plastic wrap to chill in the fridge for at least 30 minutes and up to overnight.

To make the cinnamon sugar, in a shallow bowl, mix the sugar and cinnamon until well combined.

Preheat the oven to 350°F (180°C). Line a large baking sheet with parchment paper.

Remove the dough and filling from the fridge and freezer. Scoop 2 tablespoons (30 g) of dough and flatten it into a disk. Repeat this for a total of eight disks of dough. Cover and place the remaining dough in the fridge. Pull out eight pieces of frozen Nutella. Place each piece in the center of the flattened pieces of dough. Fold the sides of the dough together to create a ball shape. Roll in your hands to create a more defined ball. Roll each of the Nutella-filled dough balls in the cinnamon sugar. Repeat with the remaining dough and Nutella filling after the first batch finishes baking. Place each of the dough balls on the baking sheet, spacing them 2 inches (5 cm) apart. Bake 10 to 12 minutes, or until the edges of the cookies are set. Keep the cookies on the hot baking sheet for 5 minutes before transferring them to a cooling rack to cool to room temperature.

cinnamon brookie bars

makes 1 (8 x 8" [20 x 20-cm]) pan

These bars are a sweet, buttery, chocolate-filled mash-up of the two most iconic baked goods: brownies and cookies. They are made from a simple fudge-like brownie layer and a buttery chocolate chip shortbread layer with hints of cinnamon spice throughout. Both the brownie and the cookie layers come together quickly and easily. Just press them into a pan, bake, slice and enjoy your new favorite cookie bar.

INGREDIENTS

for the spiced brownie layer

¼ cup (60 ml) melted unsalted butter

½ cup (85 g) milk chocolate chips

½ cup (100 g) granulated sugar

1 tsp ground instant espresso

1 tsp ground cinnamon

¼ tsp salt

1 large egg, room temperature

¼ cup (24 g) Dutch process cocoa powder

¼ tsp baking powder

½ cup (60 g) all-purpose flour

for the spiced shortbread layer

1 cup (120 g) all-purpose flour

1 tsp ground cinnamon

½ tsp salt

½ cup (113 g) unsalted butter, room temperature

½ cup (100 g) granulated sugar

1 large egg, room temperature

1 tsp vanilla extract

¾ cup (130 g) milk chocolate chips, divided

DIRECTIONS

Preheat the oven to 350°F (180°C). Lightly grease the bottom of an 8 x 8–inch (20 x 20–cm) aluminum pan and line it with parchment paper, leaving an overhang of 1 to 2 inches (2.5 to 5 cm) on two sides to allow for easy removal. Set aside.

To make the brownie layer, place the butter and chocolate chips in a microwave-safe bowl and heat in the microwave for 30 seconds. Carefully pull out the bowl. Stir the melted butter and partially melted chocolate until they are well combined. Heat in 20-second increments, stirring until the butter and chocolate are fully melted and well combined. Stir in the sugar, espresso, cinnamon and salt until smooth and well combined. Stir in the egg until smooth and well combined. Stir in the cocoa powder and baking powder until smooth and well combined. Stir in the flour until smooth and well combined. Evenly pour the brownie batter into the prepared pan. Set aside.

To make the shortbread layer, in a medium mixing bowl, whisk together the flour, cinnamon and salt until well combined. In the bowl of a stand mixer fitted with the paddle attachment, cream the butter and sugar on medium speed for 3 minutes, or until light and fluffy. Mix in the egg and vanilla until smooth and well combined. Mix the dry ingredients into the wet until just combined. Stir ½ cup (85 g) of the milk chocolate chips into the cookie dough.

Evenly top the brownie layer with pieces of the shortbread dough. This will look similar to the topping on a cobbler. Some of the brownie layer will still be visible under the cookie layer. Top the cookie layer with the remaining chocolate chips. Bake for 25 to 30 minutes. The edges of the brownie and cookie layers will be set and will pull slightly from the edges of the pan. The top of the cookie layer will be lightly golden. Cool the brookie in the pan on top of a cooling rack for 30 minutes. Remove the brookie from the pan to cool completely on the cooling rack.

peanut butter cup oatmeal skillet cookie

makes 1 (9" [23-cm]) skillet cookie

This cookie is quick and easy to make. It comes together in two bowls (or one bowl if you like), uses pantry basics and requires just a little whisking and baking time. This cozy skillet cookie has wonderfully crisp edges and a gooey center, with pockets of melted peanut butter and chocolate. The next time you need a simple and wonderfully delicious skillet cookie, this is the one to make!

INGREDIENTS

1 cup (120 g) all-purpose flour

2 tsp (6 g) ground cinnamon

½ tsp baking powder

½ tsp baking soda

½ tsp salt

½ cup (120 ml) melted unsalted butter

½ cup (100 g) light brown sugar

½ cup (100 g) granulated sugar

1 large egg, room temperature

1½ tsp (8 ml) vanilla extract

1 cup (90 g) rolled oats

½ cup (85 g) semisweet or milk chocolate chips, divided

½ cup (85 g) mini peanut butter cups or chopped full-size peanut butter cups, divided

Flaky salt, for serving (optional)

Vanilla ice cream, for serving (optional)

DIRECTIONS

Preheat the oven to 350°F (180°C). Lightly grease a 9-inch (23-cm) cast-iron skillet and set aside.

In a medium mixing bowl, whisk together the flour, cinnamon, baking powder, baking soda and salt until well combined. In a large mixing bowl, whisk the butter and sugars until well combined. Whisk in the egg and vanilla until smooth and well combined. Stir the dry ingredients into the wet until just combined with a few flour streaks. Stir in the rolled oats, ¼ cup (43 g) of the chocolate chips and ¼ cup (43 g) of the peanut butter cup pieces. Evenly spread the cookie dough into the prepared pan. Top with the remaining chocolate chips and peanut butter cup pieces.

Bake for 28 to 35 minutes, or until the edges are set and pull slightly from the edge of the skillet. The center may still look slightly underbaked, but don't worry as the cookie will continue to "bake" from the residual heat while cooling. Cool the cookie in the pan placed on a cooling rack for 30 minutes, or until the pan is cool enough to touch. Top with flaky salt and/or vanilla ice cream, if desired, right before serving.

hot chocolate cookie bars

makes 1 (9 x 13" [23 x 33–cm]) pan

There is something so cozy about a cup of hot cocoa on a cold winter day. The warmth of the rich chocolate, along with the bits of sweet, melted marshmallow pieces, is simply magical. It's a small piece of childhood in a cup. In this recipe, packets of hot chocolate are used in place of cocoa powder and marshmallow crème takes the place of the mini marshmallows. These cookie bars are nostalgic and fresh all at the same time.

INGREDIENTS

2 cups (240 g) all-purpose flour

1½ tsp (5 g) ground cinnamon

½ tsp chili powder (optional)

½ tsp baking powder

½ tsp baking soda

½ tsp salt

1 cup (226 g) unsalted butter, room temperature

1 cup (200 g) light brown sugar

½ cup (100 g) granulated sugar

½ cup (88 g) hot chocolate mix (3–4 packets of hot chocolate mix, no marshmallows)

2 large eggs, room temperature

1 large egg yolk, room temperature

2 cups (340 g) milk chocolate chips, divided

7 oz (198 g) marshmallow crème

DIRECTIONS

In a medium mixing bowl, whisk together the flour, cinnamon, chili powder (if using), baking powder, baking soda and salt. In the bowl of a stand mixer fitted with the paddle attachment, cream the butter and sugars for 4 to 5 minutes, or until light and fluffy. Beat in the hot chocolate mix until smooth and well combined. Mix in the eggs and yolk one at a time, beating well after each addition. On low, mix the dry ingredients into the wet until just combined. Fold 1¼ cups (212 g) of the milk chocolate chips into the cookie dough. Cover the dough with plastic wrap and place in the fridge for 1 hour.

Preheat the oven to 350°F (180°C). Lightly grease a 9 x 13–inch (23 x 33–cm) aluminum baking pan and line it with parchment paper, leaving an overhang of 1 to 2 inches (2.5 to 5 cm) on the two longer sides.

Roughly divide the chilled cookie dough into thirds. Reserve one-third for topping. Evenly press the remaining dough along the bottom of the baking pan. Scoop even dollops of marshmallow crème along the chilled dough. A spoon dipped in hot water can help make this easier. Spread the marshmallow crème evenly along the bottom. Top with the reserved one-third of the dough. This will not completely cover the top of the bars. The cookie dough will expand, but the marshmallow crème will still be visible on the top. Top with the remaining milk chocolate chips. Bake for 25 to 35 minutes, or until set and the edges of the cookie bars begin to pull slightly from the edge of the pan (see Tip). Cool the cookie bars in the pan on a cooling rack for 30 to 60 minutes. The bars are cool enough to eat in 30 minutes, but they will not be firm enough to lift out of the pan until closer to 1 hour. Use the overhanging parchment paper to lift and remove the bars from the pan. Slice and enjoy!

tip: At 25 to 30 minutes, the edges will be baked and the center will be slightly underbaked. For more well-baked bars, bake for 30 to 35 minutes.

chocolate pumpkin crinkle

makes 24 cookies

This recipe pairs a chocolate crinkle cookie with that irresistible pumpkin spice flavor that we all love. These cookies stay fluffy for days thanks to the addition of the pumpkin. But due to its neutral taste, the only pumpkin you'll taste is the pumpkin spice. These cookies are perfect for when you're craving a soft, pillowy, spiced, chocolate cookie that tastes as delicious as it looks!

INGREDIENTS

for the chocolate pumpkin crinkle cookies

1¾ cups (210 g) all-purpose flour

2 tsp (6 g) pumpkin spice

1½ tsp (7 g) baking powder

¼ tsp salt

5 tbsp (75 ml) melted and cooled unsalted butter

½ cup (100 g) granulated sugar

½ cup (100 g) light brown sugar

¼ cup (24 g) Dutch process cocoa powder

1 large egg, room temperature

½ cup (125 g) pumpkin puree (see tip)

1 tsp vanilla extract

for the pumpkin-spice sugar coating

½ cup (100 g) granulated sugar

1 tsp pumpkin spice

½ cup (60 g) confectioners' sugar

DIRECTIONS

To make the cookies, in a medium mixing bowl, whisk together the flour, pumpkin spice, baking powder and salt until well combined. In a separate mixing bowl, whisk together the butter and sugars until smooth and well combined. Whisk in the cocoa powder until smooth and well combined. Whisk in the egg, pumpkin puree and vanilla until smooth and well combined. Stir the dry ingredients into the wet until just combined. Cover the dough with plastic wrap, and chill it in the fridge for at least 1 hour or until the dough holds a ball shape. The dough will be very sticky even after chilling.

Make the pumpkin spice sugar by mixing the granulated sugar and pumpkin spice together in a shallow bowl. Pour the confectioners' sugar into another separate shallow bowl.

Preheat the oven to 350°F (180°C). Line two large baking sheets with parchment paper.

Scoop 1 tablespoon (15 g) of dough into your hands and roll it into a ball. Roll the ball into the spiced sugar first, coating it well. Then roll the ball in the confectioners' sugar, coating thoroughly. Place the covered dough ball onto one of the baking sheets. Repeat with the remaining dough, leaving 2 inches (5 cm) between each cookie. Bake for 11 to 12 minutes, or until the edges of the cookies are set, the center is raised and the cookies look cracked. Keep the cookies on the hot baking sheets for 5 minutes before transferring them to a cooling rack to cool to room temperature.

tip: If you'd rather skip the pumpkin, it can be replaced by 1 large egg at room temperature.

brown butter kitchen sink

makes 18-20 cookies

Some of the best meals I make at home come from throwing a bunch of delicious food together in a bowl and calling it dinner. It's with this same idea that I created these cookies. They are sweet, a little salty, soft and chewy with bits of crunchy and melty mix-ins. These cookies are perfect for customizing to your cravings.

INGREDIENTS

1¼ cups (280 g) unsalted butter

2¾ cups (330 g) all-purpose flour

1 tsp baking powder

¼ tsp baking soda

½ tsp ground cinnamon

½ tsp ground cardamom

½ tsp ground ginger

¼ tsp ground cloves

¼ tsp ground nutmeg

½ tsp salt

1 cup (200 g) light brown sugar

½ cup (100 g) granulated sugar

2 large eggs, room temperature

2 tsp (10 ml) vanilla extract

1½ cups (255 g) semisweet or milk chocolate chips (I like a mix of both)

1 cup (45 g) crushed ruffled potato chips

½ cup (15 g) coarsely chopped pretzels

¼ cup (60 g) finely chopped soft salted caramels tossed in 1 tsp flour

Flaky salt, for topping (optional)

Whole mini pretzels, for topping (optional)

DIRECTIONS

Preheat the oven to 350°F (180°C). Line two large baking sheets with parchment paper.

Melt the butter in a heavy bottom saucepan over medium heat for 7 to 10 minutes, or until the butter starts to foam. Whisk continuously until brown bits start to form. Immediately remove the pan from the heat and add to the bowl of a stand mixer fitted with the paddle attachment. Set aside to cool until warm to the touch.

In a large mixing bowl, whisk together the flour, baking powder, baking soda, cinnamon, cardamom, ginger, cloves, nutmeg and salt until well combined. Add the sugars to the butter in the stand mixer and beat on medium speed for 3 minutes. Beat in one egg on low for 20 seconds before adding the next. Beat in the vanilla. Scrape the bottom and sides of the bowl as needed. Beat the ingredients together for 2 to 3 minutes, or until lighter in color and slightly thickened. With the mixer on low, add the dry ingredients to the wet until just combined. Scrape down the bottom and sides of the bowl as needed. With the mixer on low, mix in the chocolate chips. By hand, fold in the potato chips, pretzels and caramels.

Scoop 3-tablespoon (45-g) amounts of the cookie dough onto the baking sheets, spacing them 3 inches (8 cm) apart. Bake for 12 to 16 minutes, or until they are lightly golden with set edges and very fragrant. Keep the cookies on the hot baking sheets for 5 minutes before transferring them to a cooling rack to cool to room temperature. Top with flaky salt, if using, and a mini pretzel in the center, if using.

tips: These cookies will spread while baking. While the cookies are still hot from the oven, use a large biscuit or cookie cutter that's wider than the cookies to help shape any cookies into a rounder shape. These cookies are technically no-chill; however, the flavors and texture of the cookie are even better with a little time in the fridge. One hour of chill time is recommended, but not required.

autumn-spiced double chocolate

makes 24 cookies

Chocolate fans, this is your cookie! These have crisp edges and gooey centers and are filled with delicious chocolate flavor. The blend of cinnamon, cloves and nutmeg is the perfect balance to the strong cocoa notes of the cookies. For this cookie, I love milk chocolate chips or chunks to bring a bit of sweet, milky brightness to contrast the deeper chocolate flavor of the cookie.

INGREDIENTS

1¾ cups (210 g) all-purpose flour

2 tsp (6 g) ground cinnamon

½ tsp ground cloves or allspice

¼ tsp ground nutmeg

¾ tsp baking soda

½ tsp salt

1 cup (240 ml) melted unsalted butter

½ cup (48 g) unsweetened cocoa powder

1¼ cups (250 g) light brown sugar

¼ cup (50 g) granulated sugar

1 large egg, room temperature

1 large egg yolk, room temperature

2 cups (340 g) semisweet or milk chocolate chips or chunks

DIRECTIONS

In a medium mixing bowl, whisk together the flour, cinnamon, cloves, nutmeg, baking soda and salt until well combined. In the bowl of a stand mixer fitted with the paddle attachment, beat the melted butter and cocoa powder on medium speed until smooth and well combined. Beat in the sugars on medium speed until smooth and well combined. Beat in the egg and egg yolk until smooth and well combined. Scrape the bottom and sides of the bowl as needed. Mix on low for 1 minute. With the mixer on low, mix the dry ingredients into the wet until just combined. Fold in the chocolate chips. Cover the dough with plastic wrap, and chill it in the fridge for at least 1 hour and up to overnight.

Preheat the oven to 350°F (180°C). Line two large baking sheets with parchment paper. Pull the cookie dough from the fridge to sit at room temperature for 20 minutes before baking.

Scoop 2-tablespoon (30-g) amounts of the cookie dough onto the baking sheets, spacing them 3 inches (8 cm) apart. These cookies will spread quite a bit while baking. Bake for 12 to 14 minutes, or until the edges are set with slightly puffed centers. Keep the cookies on the hot baking sheets for 5 minutes before transferring them to a cooling rack to cool to room temperature.

tip: Reshape these cookies by nudging the edges back into a circular shape using a large, circular cookie cutter or pastry ring. Read more about this technique on page 10.

pumpkin chocolate chip

makes 16 cookies

Pumpkin and chocolate are a truly delicious combination. So, naturally, I wanted to incorporate pumpkin into my favorite classic cookie. These are buttery and chewy, while still retaining that unmistakable texture of pumpkin. They are flavored with just enough pumpkin spice to tame the sweetness of the chocolate chips.

INGREDIENTS

for the brown butter

1 cup + 2 tbsp (254 g) unsalted butter

for the pumpkin chocolate chip cookies

½ cup (125 g) pumpkin puree

2 cups (240 g) all-purpose flour

2 tsp (6 g) pumpkin spice

1 tsp baking soda

¼ tsp baking powder

½ tsp salt

¾ cup (150 g) light brown sugar

¼ cup (50 g) granulated sugar

1 large egg yolk

1 tsp vanilla extract

2 cups (340 g) semisweet or milk chocolate chips or chunks

DIRECTIONS

Melt the butter in a heavy bottom saucepan over medium heat for 7 to 10 minutes, or until the butter starts to foam. Whisk continuously until brown bits start to form. Depending on your stove and saucepan, the entire process should take 10 to 15 minutes. Immediately remove the pan from the heat, and pour the brown butter into the mixing bowl of a stand mixer fitted with the paddle attachment to cool slightly. Lay two or three paper towels across a wide, shallow bowl. Scoop the pumpkin puree onto the paper towels. The excess water will absorb into the paper towels. Before using in the recipe, squeeze the excess water from the pumpkin.

In a medium mixing bowl, whisk together the flour, pumpkin spice, baking soda, baking powder and salt until well combined. Add the sugars to the stand mixer bowl with the butter, and beat on medium speed until smooth and well combined. Beat in the egg yolk, blotted pumpkin puree and vanilla until smooth and well combined. Scrape the bottom and sides of the bowl as needed. Mix on low for 1 minute. With the mixer on low, mix the dry ingredients into the wet until just combined. Fold in the chocolate chips. Cover the dough with plastic wrap, and chill it in the fridge for at least 8 hours and up to 2 days.

Pull the cookie dough from the fridge to sit at room temperature for 30 minutes before baking. Preheat the oven to 375°F (190°C). Line two large baking sheets with parchment paper.

Scoop 3-tablespoon (45-g) amounts of the cookie dough onto the baking sheets, spacing them 3 inches (8 cm) apart. Bake for 10 to 12 minutes, or until the cookies have set with golden brown edges and centers that are a light golden brown. Keep the cookies on the hot baking sheets for 5 minutes before transferring them to a cooling rack to cool to room temperature.

espresso and chocolate neapolitan

makes 16 cookies

These are the first cookies I created for this chapter. Chocolate and espresso share many similar flavor notes, which makes them perfect for pairing together in a spiced sugar cookie. The inspiration for these cookies comes from the talented Sarah Kieffer. While the cookies do take a little time to assemble, the results are so fun and more than worth the time.

INGREDIENTS

for the spiced espresso and chocolate neapolitan cookies

2¼ cups (270 g) all-purpose flour

2 tsp (5 g) cornstarch

2 tsp (6 g) ground cinnamon

½ tsp baking soda

½ tsp salt

1 cup (226 g) unsalted butter, room temperature

1¼ cups (250 g) granulated sugar

1 large egg, room temperature

1 large egg yolk, room temperature

2 tsp (10 ml) vanilla extract

1 tbsp (6 g) instant espresso powder

1 tbsp (6 g) Dutch processed cocoa powder

for the spiced sugar

¼ cup (50 g) granulated sugar

1 tsp ground cinnamon

DIRECTIONS

To make the cookies, in a medium mixing bowl, whisk together the flour, cornstarch, cinnamon, baking soda and salt until well combined. In the bowl of a stand mixer fitted with the paddle attachment, cream the butter and sugar on medium speed for 3 minutes. Scrape the bottom and sides of the mixing bowl as needed. On low, beat in the egg, egg yolk and vanilla until smooth and well combined. With the mixer on the lowest setting, mix the dry ingredients into the wet until just combined.

Divide the dough into three equal groups. Pat one dough piece into a disk shape. Wrap in plastic wrap and store in the fridge. This is the cinnamon dough. Return the second piece of cookie dough to the bowl of the stand mixer. Add the instant espresso powder. Mix on low until fully combined. Form the cookie dough into a disk, wrap in plastic wrap and store in the fridge. This is the espresso dough. Add the last piece of dough to the bowl of the stand mixer along with the cocoa powder. Mix on low until fully combined. Form the cookie dough into a disk, wrap in plastic wrap and store in the fridge. This is the chocolate dough. All three pieces of cookie dough should chill in the fridge for at least 1 hour and up to overnight.

Preheat the oven to 350°F (180°C). Line two large baking sheets with parchment paper. Pull out the three cookie doughs.

To make the spiced sugar, in a shallow bowl, mix the sugar and cinnamon until well combined. Scoop 1-tablespoon (15-g) amounts of the cinnamon dough, forming 15 to 16 cookie dough balls on the baking sheets. Space each ball 3 inches (8 cm) apart. Repeat with the espresso dough, placing each cookie ball next to a cinnamon cookie ball. Repeat with the chocolate dough. You should end up with 15 to 16 groups of dough balls, each with the three flavors. Take one group of dough balls and gently press them together to form one large ball of cookie dough. Roll the ball through the spiced sugar and place it on a baking sheet. Repeat for all the remaining cookie dough groups, spacing each of the large cookie dough balls 3 inches (8 cm) apart. Bake for 11 to 12 minutes, or until the edges are set and the entire cookie looks slightly puffed. Once baked, place the hot pans on cooling racks until they cool to room temperature.

pumpkin-spiced chocolate pinwheels

makes 24 cookies

These cookies are made from a buttery, orange-spiced sugar cookie dough that gets divided into two fun flavors: chocolate and chocolate chip. They are then layered and rolled together to form a swirl or pinwheel pattern. These slice-and-bake cookies are as fun to eat as they are to look at!

INGREDIENTS

3 cups (360 g) all-purpose flour

1 tbsp (9 g) pumpkin spice

¾ tsp baking powder

½ tsp salt

1 cup (226 g) unsalted butter, room temperature

1 cup (200 g) granulated sugar

¼ cup (50 g) light brown sugar

1 large egg, room temperature

2 tsp (10 ml) vanilla extract

½ cup (85 g) mini chocolate chips

2 tbsp (12 g) Dutch process cocoa powder

DIRECTIONS

In a medium mixing bowl, whisk together the flour, pumpkin spice, baking powder and salt until well combined. In the bowl of a stand mixer fitted with the paddle attachment, beat the butter and sugars on medium speed for 3 to 4 minutes, or until light, fluffy and well combined. Scrape the bottom and sides of the bowl as needed. On low speed, mix in the egg and vanilla until well combined. Scrape the bottom and sides of the bowl as needed. Mix for 30 seconds. On low speed, mix the dry ingredients into the wet until just combined.

Roughly divide the dough into two pieces. Place one dough ball onto a large piece of parchment paper. Leave the other half of the dough in the mixer. With the mixer on low, fold in the mini chocolate chips. Transfer the dough from the bowl onto another piece of parchment paper. Place the second dough ball into the mixing bowl. Mix in the cocoa powder until well combined. Transfer the dough back onto the same piece of parchment paper it was on before. Place a large piece of plastic wrap on top of one of the dough balls. Roll the dough into a rectangle that's ¼ inch (6 mm) thick. Repeat with the remaining cookie dough with another piece of plastic wrap. Transfer the rectangles onto a small baking sheet or very large plate to chill in the fridge for 30 minutes.

Place the chocolate chip rectangle on top of the chocolate rectangle, cover with plastic wrap and roll out the layered cookie dough to measure 11 x 13 inches (28 x 33 cm). Using the parchment paper as a guide, roll up the rectangles into a log along the long side of the dough. Place the log back onto the baking sheet or large plate. Loosely cover the log with plastic wrap. Chill it in the fridge for 2 hours or until the dough is very firm.

Preheat the oven to 350°F (180°C). Line two baking sheets with parchment paper.

Slice the dough into ½-inch (1.3-cm)-thick cookies. Place each cookie onto the baking sheets, spacing them 2 inches (5 cm) apart. Bake for 11 to 12 minutes, or until the edges are set. Keep the cookies on the hot baking sheet for 5 minutes before transferring them to a cooling rack to cool to room temperature.

Nuts
creamy, buttery and earthy

Did you know that some commonly known nuts are not actually tree nuts? Almonds, cashews and pistachios are technically known as drupes in botanical terms; macadamia nuts and pine nuts are seeds; and peanuts are legumes (in the bean family). They all tend to have a nutty flavor and texture, which is why they tend to be grouped together; however, differences in flavor such as sweetness and creaminess can vary quite a bit from one type of "nut" to another. This chapter will help you discover all the nuanced flavors and textures that different types of nuts can bring to a cookie.

Hazelnuts have a woody and nutty taste, which balances sweet flavors such as chocolate. Taste this classic and delicious combination in the Chocolate Hazelnut Butter Sandwich Cookies (page 89). Pecans have a sweet, nutty and buttery flavor that pairs beautifully with cinnamon and citrus as found in the Spiced Mexican Wedding Cookies (page 84). Some recipes call for toasting the nuts prior to using them in the recipe. This helps enhance and release their natural flavors. If you have the time, toasting the nuts is a fantastic flavor boost, but unless the recipe specifically calls for toasting, it remains optional.

maple pecan pie shortbread bars

makes 1 (9 x 13" [23 x 33–cm]) pan

I really wanted to make a festive cookie bar that could be enjoyed by a gathering of friends and family for holidays and celebrations. These bars are my "no-fuss" version of pecan pie bars and fit the festive cookie bar goal so perfectly. They're sweet, but not too sweet, wonderfully buttery and generously spiced. They're the perfect cross between a cookie bar and pie.

INGREDIENTS

for the spiced shortbread base

1 cup (226 g) unsalted butter, room temperature

½ cup (100 g) granulated sugar

2 tsp (6 g) ground cinnamon

1 tsp vanilla extract

½ tsp salt

2 cups (240 g) all-purpose flour

for the spiced maple pecan pie filling

¼ cup (60 ml) melted unsalted butter

¾ cup (150 g) maple sugar or light brown sugar

½ cup (120 ml) maple syrup

2 tsp (10 ml) vanilla extract

2 tsp (6 g) ground cinnamon

½ tsp salt

2 eggs, room temperature

2 cups (225 g) roughly chopped pecans

DIRECTIONS

Preheat the oven to 350°F (180°C). Lightly grease a 9 x 13–inch (23 x 33–cm) aluminum pan and line it with parchment paper, leaving an overhang of 2 inches (5 cm) on two sides to allow for easy removal.

To make the shortbread base, place the butter, sugar, cinnamon, vanilla and salt in the bowl of a stand mixer fitted with the paddle attachment. Cream on medium speed for 3 to 4 minutes, or until well combined. Scrape the bottom and sides of the bowl as needed. On low speed, mix in the flour in two batches, until just combined. Scrape the bottom and sides of the bowl between each flour addition to help incorporate any stray pieces. Scoop even pieces of the cookie dough into the prepared pan. Press the dough into the corners and across the pan in an even layer. Bake on the center rack for 20 minutes, or until the shortbread is set. Cool on a cooling rack while you prepare the maple pecan pie filling.

To make the filling, in a medium mixing bowl, whisk together the butter, sugar, maple syrup, vanilla, cinnamon and salt until smooth and well combined. Whisk in the eggs until smooth and well combined. Fold in the pecans. Pour the mixture on top of the warm shortbread base. Bake for 20 to 25 minutes, or until the filling is baked through, the edges are completely set and the center gives a slight jiggle. The internal temperature should read 200°F (95°C).

Cool the bars in the pan placed on a cooling rack for 1 to 2 hours or until fully cooled. Run a butter knife along the edges of the pan while it's still warm to loosen any bits of filling that may be stuck to the pan. Remove the bars from the pan using the overhanging parchment paper, slice and enjoy. Store leftover shortbread bars in an airtight container in the fridge.

tip: To make this recipe in a smaller amount, halve the ingredients and bake in an 8 x 8–inch (20 x 20–cm) pan.

spiced mexican wedding cookies

makes 32 cookies

I absolutely love Mexican wedding cookies. There's something so completely delicious about a simple buttery cookie coated in confectioners' sugar. These are full of toasted, buttery pecan flavor that pairs perfectly with sweet and spicy cinnamon and bright orange zest. Once they're coated in confectioners' sugar, they are absolutely divine. In fact, they are my favorite cookie in this chapter.

INGREDIENTS

1 cup (95 g) pecans

2¼ cups (270 g) all-purpose flour

1 tsp ground cinnamon

½ tsp baking powder

¼ tsp salt

1 cup (226 g) unsalted butter, room temperature

1½ cups (180 g) confectioners' sugar, divided

Zest of 1 medium orange

1 tsp vanilla extract

½ tsp almond extract

DIRECTIONS

Place the pecans in a small skillet, and lightly toast them over medium-low heat for 4 to 5 minutes, or until fragrant. Transfer the pecans to a food processor. Process until the pecans are fine like the texture of almond flour. Cool slightly before using in the recipe. In a medium mixing bowl, whisk together the flour, cinnamon, baking powder and salt until well combined. Add the butter, ¾ cup (90 g) of the confectioners' sugar and zest in the bowl of a stand mixer fitted with the paddle attachment. On medium speed, beat the mixture for 3 to 4 minutes, or until light and fluffy. Scrape the bottom and sides of the bowl as needed. On low speed, mix in the ground pecans and vanilla and almond extracts until smooth and well combined. Scrape the bottom and sides of the bowl as needed. On low, mix the dry ingredients into the wet until well combined. Wrap the dough in plastic wrap, and chill it in the fridge for 30 minutes.

Preheat the oven to 350°F (180°C). Line two large baking sheets with parchment paper.

Scoop 1-tablespoon (15-g) amounts of the cookie dough onto the baking sheets, spacing them 2 inches (5 cm) apart. Bake for 10 to 12 minutes, or until the edges are lightly golden brown. Cool the cookies on the hot baking sheet for 15 minutes. While the cookies are still slightly warm, roll them in the remaining confectioners' sugar. Cool completely to room temperature and roll them once more in the confectioners' sugar if you would like a double coat of sugar.

bourbon pecan thumbprints

makes 28 cookies

There are few flavor pairings in the South that are as classic as pecans, bourbon and vanilla. Playing off these complementary flavors, I wanted to create a cookie that is as much fun to make as it is to eat. These cookies are buttery, chewy, salty and sweet. The hints of bourbon and vanilla pair so deliciously well with the salted caramel filling.

INGREDIENTS

for the bourbon pecan thumbprint cookies

2 cups (190 g) pecans

1 large egg, room temperature, divided

2 cups (240 g) all-purpose flour

1 tbsp (9 g) ground cinnamon

½ tsp salt

1 cup (226 g) cubed unsalted butter, cold

½ cup (100 g) granulated sugar

½ cup (100 g) light brown sugar

1 tsp vanilla extract

2 tbsp (30 ml) bourbon

DIRECTIONS

To make the cookies, process the pecans in a food processor until they resemble coarse sand or the texture of almond flour. Divide the pecans into two bowls, with ½ cup (48 g) in one bowl and 1½ cups (142 g) in the other. Set the bowls aside.

Line a large plate or small baking sheet with parchment or wax paper. This is just for chilling the cookie dough balls and will not be used for baking. Into two small bowls, separate the egg yolk from the white. The yolk will get mixed into the batter, while the white will be used to coat the cookies before rolling in the ground pecans.

In a medium mixing bowl, whisk together the flour, cinnamon and salt until well combined. In the bowl of a stand mixer fitted with the paddle attachment, cream the butter for 2 to 3 minutes, or until smooth. With the mixer on low, stream in the sugars, and then beat on medium-low speed until well combined. Increase the mixing speed to medium for 1 minute. Scrape the bottom and sides of the bowl as needed. On low, mix in the ½ cup (48 g) of ground pecans until well combined. Mix in the egg yolk, vanilla and the bourbon until smooth and well combined. On low, mix the dry ingredients into the wet until just combined. Scrape the bottom and sides of the bowl as needed.

Scoop 1 tablespoon (15 g) of the cookie dough and roll it into a smooth ball with your hands. Dip the cookie dough ball into the egg whites, making sure to completely cover the dough. Roll the coated dough into the remaining ground pecans. Place the coated cookie dough ball onto the lined plate or baking sheet. Repeat for the remaining dough. Use a wine cork, your thumb or the back of a teaspoon measuring spoon to create an indentation in the center of each cookie. Place the cookie dough in the fridge to chill for 30 minutes.

(continued)

bourbon pecan thumbprints (continued)

for the caramel filling
1 cup (200 g) granulated sugar
6 tbsp (85 g) unsalted butter
⅔ cup (160 ml) heavy cream
½ tsp salt

for the topping
28 whole pecans
Flaky salt

Preheat the oven to 350°F (180°C). Line two large baking sheets with parchment paper.

To make the filling, place the sugar in a small saucepan and heat it over medium-low heat. Once the sugar begins to melt, stir it continuously until fully melted. Stop stirring and whisk in the butter. Once the butter has fully melted into the sugar, leave the mixture to cook for 1 minute. Slowly pour and stir in the heavy cream. The mixture will bubble up. Remove the pan from the heat. Stir in the salt until fully incorporated. Pour the hot caramel sauce into a heatproof container to cool to room temperature while you bake the cookies.

Place each of the dough balls on the baking sheets, spacing them 2 inches (5 cm) apart. Bake for 12 to 14 minutes, or until the edges of the cookies are set and a light golden brown color. Cool the cookies on the sheets placed on top of a cooling rack for 5 minutes. During this time, use the wine cork or teaspoon to remake the indentation. Transfer the cookies to a cooling rack to completely cool to room temperature. Fill each indentation with 1 to 1½ teaspoons (5 to 8 ml) of caramel sauce. Press a whole pecan into the caramel and sprinkle with flaky salt.

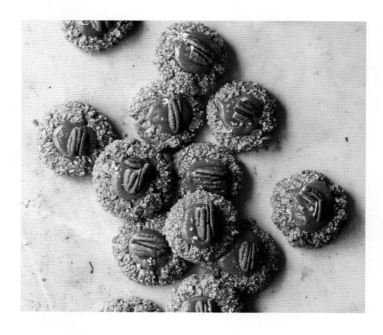

chocolate hazelnut butter sandwich cookies
makes 16–17 sandwich cookies

I took my inspiration for this cookie from two iconic foods: Nutella and Oreo cookies. This recipe is my delicious mash-up of the two. Nutty and spiced chocolate cookies are sandwiched together with a sweet hazelnut buttercream. For an extra special decorative touch, top the cookies with melted milk chocolate and crushed hazelnuts.

INGREDIENTS

for the hazelnut butter

2 cups (230 g) hazelnuts

3 tbsp (38 g) granulated sugar

1 tsp ground cinnamon

½ tsp salt

for the spiced hazelnut chocolate cookies

1¾ cups (210 g) all-purpose flour, plus more as needed

1 tsp ground cinnamon

¼ tsp ground cloves

1 tsp baking powder

¼ tsp salt

½ cup (113 g) unsalted butter, room temperature

¾ cup (150 g) light brown sugar

¼ cup (50 g) granulated sugar

½ cup (115 g) prepared hazelnut butter from above

1 tsp instant espresso powder

¼ cup (24 g) Dutch process cocoa powder

1 large egg, room temperature

4 oz (113 g) milk chocolate, melted

½ cup (58 g) finely chopped hazelnuts

DIRECTIONS

To make the hazelnut butter, add the hazelnuts, sugar, cinnamon and salt to a food processor, and process until smooth like a nut butter. The hazelnut butter will be divided into two different parts for the recipe. Each part will require ½ cup (115 g) of hazelnut butter. If you have any extra hazelnut butter, it lasts up to 1 month when stored in the fridge in an airtight container.

To make the cookies, in a medium mixing bowl, whisk together the flour, cinnamon, cloves, baking powder and salt until well combined. In the bowl of a stand mixer fitted with the paddle attachment, cream the butter, sugars and prepared hazelnut butter on medium speed for 4 to 5 minutes, or until well combined. Scrape the bottom and sides of the bowl as needed. On low, mix in the espresso powder and cocoa powder until smooth and well combined. Scrape the bottom and sides of the bowl as needed. Mix in the egg until smooth and well combined. With the mixer on low, mix the dry ingredients into the wet until just combined. If the dough feels too sticky, mix in 2 to 3 tablespoons (15 to 23 g) of additional flour until the dough feels tacky.

Divide the dough into two equal pieces. Drop half of the dough onto a large piece of parchment paper. Place a large piece of plastic wrap over the top and roll the dough out until it's ¼ inch (6 mm) thick. Fully wrap the dough in the plastic wrap. Repeat for the remaining dough ball. Place the cookie dough in the fridge to chill for at least 2 hours and up to overnight.

(continued)

chocolate hazelnut butter sandwich cookies (continued)

for the hazelnut buttercream

½ cup (113 g) unsalted butter, room temperature

½ cup (115 g) prepared hazelnut butter

1 tsp vanilla extract

¼ tsp salt

2 cups (240 g) confectioners' sugar, divided

1 tbsp (15 ml) milk, plus more as needed

Preheat the oven to 350°F (180°C). Line two large baking sheets with parchment paper.

Remove one sheet of chilled dough. Unwrap the dough and place it onto a piece of parchment paper. Using a small 2-inch (5-cm) biscuit or cookie cutter, cut out rounds of chilled dough. For any excess dough, gently gather the excess dough, roll it back into a ball in plastic wrap, chill in the fridge until it can hold its shape, and then roll out and cut again; repeat until all the dough is used up. Gently lift the cut pieces onto the baking sheets. Space the cookies 2 inches (5 cm) apart. They shouldn't spread too much while baking. While the first batch of cookies bakes, pull out the second dough sheet and repeat the process.

Bake the cookies for 9 to 11 minutes, or until the edges are set. Keep the cookies on the hot baking sheets for 5 minutes before transferring them to a cooling rack to cool to room temperature. Drizzle the melted chocolate on top of one half of the cookies (these will be the tops of the sandwiches). Sprinkle the finely chopped hazelnuts on top of the wet chocolate. Let the chocolate set for at least 45 minutes.

While the cookies set, make the hazelnut buttercream. In the bowl of a stand mixer fitted with the paddle attachment, cream the butter and prepared hazelnut butter on medium speed until smooth and well combined. On low, mix in the vanilla, salt and 1 cup (120 g) of confectioners' sugar until smooth and well combined. With the mixer on low, add in the remaining 1 cup (120 g) sugar and the milk. Mix on medium speed until all the ingredients are smooth and well combined. If the buttercream is too thick, add 1 teaspoon of milk at a time up to 1 tablespoon (15 ml), until the buttercream is your desired consistency. If the buttercream is too warm to apply to the cookies, chill it in the fridge.

To assemble, apply the desired amount of buttercream to the bottom of the plain cookies using a 1-tablespoon (15-g) cookie scoop or piping bag with the tip of your choice. Place the chocolate-drizzled cookie on top of the frosting side of the bottom cookie and gently press together.

milk chocolate cashew

makes 24 cookies

These cookies are thin, buttery and nutty, with a heavenly filling of sweet milk chocolate. While baking, these cookies are meant to spread and develop lots of ripples with crisp edges. They are the salty-sweet milk chocolate cookie you'll bake over and over again.

INGREDIENTS

1 cup (146 g) raw, unsalted whole cashews

1½ cups (180 g) all-purpose flour

2 tsp (6 g) ground cinnamon

1 tsp baking powder

1½ tsp (7 g) baking soda

1 tsp salt

1 cup (226 g) unsalted butter, room temperature

1 cup (200 g) light brown sugar

½ cup (100 g) granulated sugar

2 large eggs, room temperature

2 tsp (10 ml) vanilla extract

12 oz (340 g) milk chocolate, evenly chopped, divided

Flaky salt (optional)

DIRECTIONS

Process the cashews in a food processor until the nuts resemble coarse sand or the texture of almond flour. Set aside. In a medium mixing bowl, whisk together the flour, cinnamon, baking powder, baking soda and salt until well combined.

In the bowl of a stand mixer fitted with the paddle attachment, beat the butter and sugars on medium speed for 3 minutes, or until light and fluffy. Scrape the bottom and sides of the bowl as needed. On low, beat in the finely ground cashews until creamy and well combined. Beat in the eggs and vanilla until smooth and well combined. On low, stir the dry ingredients into the wet until just combined. Fold in 9 ounces (255 g) of the milk chocolate pieces. Cover the dough with plastic wrap and chill it in the fridge for at least 2 hours. The cookies can be stored this way for up to 2 days.

Preheat the oven to 375°F (190°C). Line two large baking sheets with parchment paper.

Scoop 2-tablespoon (30-g) amounts of the cookie dough onto the baking sheets, spacing them 3 inches (8 cm) apart. Top the cookie dough with the remaining pieces of chopped chocolate. Bake for 9 to 11 minutes, or until the edges of the cookies are set and golden brown. Keep the cookies on the hot baking sheet for 5 minutes before transferring them to a cooling rack to cool to room temperature. Sprinkle with flaky salt, if you like, before serving.

salted honey nut bars

makes 1 (9 x 13" [23 x 33-cm]) pan

One of the simplest and most delicious snacks I love to make is toast with butter, honey and a pinch of salt. I love the contrast of the sweet floral honey against the creaminess of the butter, balanced out with the salt. Occasionally, I also like to chop up whichever nuts I happen to be craving at the time. That simple snack is what inspired these cookie bars. They are made from a buttery, lemon-scented sugar cookie base and topped with a spiced honey nut filling made from a blend of walnuts and pistachios. As the filling bakes, it takes on a sweet, caramelized texture that is out-of-this-world delicious. Unlike similar fillings that are prepared with eggs, these cookie bars can be stored and enjoyed at room temperature.

INGREDIENTS

for the cookie crust
1¾ cups (210 g) all-purpose flour

¼ cup (28 g) almond flour

2 tbsp (20 g) cornstarch

1 cup (200 g) granulated sugar

Zest of 1 lemon

¾ cup (170 g) unsalted butter, room temperature

1 large egg yolk, room temperature

1 tsp vanilla extract

for the salted honey nut filling
½ cup (113 g) unsalted butter

½ cup (100 g) light brown sugar

½ cup (120 ml) honey

1 tbsp (15 ml) lemon juice

1 tbsp (9 g) ground cinnamon

1 tsp salt

1½ cups (185 g) finely chopped raw walnuts

1 cup (100 g) finely chopped raw pistachios

DIRECTIONS

Preheat the oven to 350°F (180°C). Lightly grease the bottom of a 9 x 13–inch (23 x 33–cm) aluminum pan and line it with parchment paper, leaving an overhang of 2 inches (5 cm) on two sides to allow for easy removal.

To make the crust, in a medium mixing bowl, whisk together the all-purpose flour, almond flour and cornstarch until well combined. In the bowl of a stand mixer fitted with the paddle attachment, add the sugar and zest, and on low speed, mix until the texture resembles wet sand. Beat in the butter on medium speed for 3 to 4 minutes, or until light and fluffy. Scrape the bottom and sides of the bowl as needed. Mix in the egg yolk and vanilla until smooth and well combined. On low speed, mix the dry ingredients into the wet until just combined. If needed, use a spatula or your hands to work any stray pieces into the dough. Evenly press the dough into the prepared pan. Bake for 15 minutes, or until the edges are lightly golden brown and the top is set. Cool the crust in the pan while you prepare the filling.

To make the filling, place the butter, brown sugar, honey and lemon juice in a small saucepan, and heat over medium heat until the sugar fully dissolves. Bring the mixture to a boil for 2 minutes. Remove from the heat, stir in the cinnamon, salt, walnuts and pistachios.

Pour the sweetened nut mixture on top of the cookie crust. Bake for 25 to 30 minutes, or until the top is bubbling and is golden brown in color. Remove the pan to cool on a cooling rack for 1 hour or until room temperature. Within the first 15 to 30 minutes, run a butter knife along the unlined sides of the pan to loosen any filling that may have baked onto the pan. Once the cookie bars are completely cooled, remove from the pan using the overhanging parchment paper, slice and enjoy!

nutella swirl peanut butter

makes 20 cookies

It wouldn't be a cookie book without a peanut butter cookie recipe. However, I didn't want to make just any kind of peanut butter cookie—I wanted it to look as good as it tastes! I happened to have some Nutella left over from another cookie recipe and decided to swirl it into the peanut butter cookie dough. I am so glad I did, because it makes for a phenomenal cookie. If you're a fan of the tagalong cookies sold every spring, you will absolutely love these.

INGREDIENTS

2¼ cups (270 g) all-purpose flour

2 tsp (6 g) ground cinnamon

½ tsp baking soda

½ tsp baking powder

½ tsp salt

1 cup (226 g) unsalted butter, room temperature

1¼ cups (250 g) light brown sugar

¼ cup (50 g) granulated sugar

¾ cup (192 g) creamy peanut butter

2 large eggs, room temperature

2 tsp (10 ml) vanilla extract

1 cup (320 g) chocolate-hazelnut spread (I prefer Nutella brand), divided

DIRECTIONS

Line a small baking sheet or large plate with parchment paper. This will be used to hold the scooped cookie dough while it chills.

In a medium mixing bowl, whisk together the flour, cinnamon, baking soda, baking powder and salt. In the bowl of a stand mixer fitted with the paddle attachment, beat the butter and sugars together on medium speed for 4 to 5 minutes, or until well combined. Scrape the bottom and sides of the bowl as needed. On medium speed, beat in the peanut butter until smooth and well combined. On low speed, mix in the eggs and vanilla until smooth and well combined. Scrape the bottom and sides of the bowl as needed. With the mixer on low, mix the dry ingredients into the wet until just combined.

We're going to incorporate the Nutella into the dough in two batches. First, drop ½ cup (160 g) of the Nutella in big dollops on top of the cookie dough and gently swirl it in. Scoop 3-tablespoon (45-g) balls of Nutella-swirled cookie dough onto the baking sheet or plate. Once the first half of the dough is scooped, drop the remaining Nutella onto the remaining dough, swirl it in and scoop the dough. When all the dough is scooped onto the baking sheet or plate, loosely cover the cookies with plastic wrap. Chill them in the fridge for 45 to 60 minutes, or until they can easily be rolled into a ball.

Preheat the oven to 350°F (180°C). Line two large baking sheets with parchment paper.

Gently roll the scooped cookie dough into balls with your hands and place them onto the baking sheets, spacing them 2 inches (5 cm) apart. Bake for 10 to 12 minutes, or until the edges are set. Keep the cookies on the hot baking sheets for 5 minutes before transferring them to a cooling rack to cool to room temperature.

pb and j thumbprints

makes 28 cookies

Peanut butter and jelly sandwiches are as classic Americana as it gets. Turns out PB and J makes a fantastic cookie too! These thumbprints are made from a sweet peanut butter cookie base, rolled in crushed salted peanuts and filled with a homemade strawberry jam. If you're pressed for time, a good-quality preserve works nicely as well.

INGREDIENTS

for the strawberry jam

1 lb (454 g) strawberries, quartered

1 cup (200 g) granulated sugar

½ cup (120 ml) water

¼ tsp ground coriander (see tip)

for the peanut butter thumbprint cookies

1 large egg, room temperature

1 cup (146 g) finely chopped salted peanuts

1¾ cups (210 g) all-purpose flour

2 tsp (6 g) ground cinnamon

½ tsp salt

½ cup (113 g) unsalted butter, room temperature

½ cup (100 g) granulated sugar

½ cup (100 g) light brown sugar

½ cup (128 g) creamy peanut butter

1 tsp vanilla extract

> tip: While coriander may seem like an odd choice to pair with strawberries, the chemical properties of this particular spice enhance the flavor of the strawberries. You can omit if you'd like.

DIRECTIONS

To make the jam, in a medium saucepan or skillet over medium heat, bring the strawberries, sugar, water and coriander to a boil. Reduce to a simmer and cook for 20 to 25 minutes. The jam should easily coat the back of a spoon and measure approximately 1 cup (240 ml). Cool to room temperature before using in the recipe. Meanwhile, line a small baking sheet or large plate with parchment paper for chilling the dough.

To make the cookies, into two small bowls, separate the egg into the yolk and whites. Place the peanuts in a separate bowl. In a medium mixing bowl, whisk together the flour, cinnamon and salt until well combined. In the bowl of a stand mixer fitted with the paddle attachment, beat the butter and sugars together on medium speed for 3 to 4 minutes, or until light, fluffy and well combined. Beat in the peanut butter until well combined. Scrape the bottom and sides of the bowl as needed. On low, beat in the egg yolk and vanilla, and then mix the dry ingredients into the wet until just combined. Scrape the bottom and sides of the bowl as needed.

Scoop 1 tablespoon (15 g) of the cookie dough and roll it into a smooth ball using your hands. Roll the dough ball into the egg whites, and then into the peanuts. Place the coated cookie dough ball onto the lined baking sheet or plate. Repeat for the remaining dough. Use a wine cork, your thumb or the back of a teaspoon measuring spoon and create an indentation in the center of each cookie. Place the cookie dough in the fridge to chill for 30 to 60 minutes. The cookies should be cold and firm before baking.

Preheat the oven to 350°F (180°C). Line two large baking sheets with parchment paper. Place each of the dough balls on the baking sheet 2 inches (5 cm) apart. Bake the cookies for 12 to 14 minutes, or until the edges are set and a light golden brown color. Keep the cookies on the hot baking sheet for 5 minutes. Use the wine cork or teaspoon to remake the indentations. Then, transfer the cookies to a cooling rack to completely cool to room temperature. Fill each indentation with ½ to 1 teaspoon of the homemade strawberry jam.

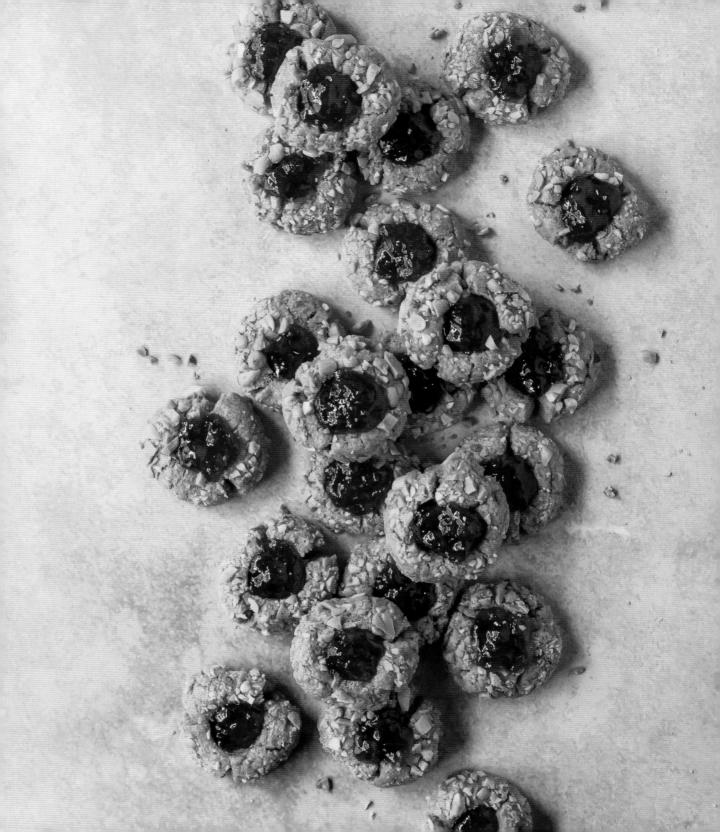

spiced almond

makes 30 cookies

These are soft and delicate two-bite cookies. The blend of bright spices works well to balance the slightly floral notes of the almond extract. The sweet almond glaze and sliced almonds are a simple and elegant way to finish the cookies.

INGREDIENTS

for the spiced almond cookies

2 cups (240 g) all-purpose flour

¼ cup (28 g) almond flour

½ tsp salt

¼ tsp baking powder

¼ tsp ground cardamom

¼ tsp ground cinnamon

¼ tsp ground cloves

1 cup (226 g) unsalted butter, room temperature

¾ cup (150 g) granulated sugar

2 tsp (10 ml) almond extract

for the almond glaze

1½ cups (180 g) confectioners' sugar

½ tsp almond extract

1 tbsp (15 ml) water, plus more as needed

½ cup (60 g) sliced almonds

DIRECTIONS

Preheat the oven to 375°F (190°C). Line two large baking sheets with parchment paper.

To make the cookies, in a medium mixing bowl, whisk together the all-purpose flour, almond flour, salt, baking powder, cardamom, cinnamon and cloves. In the bowl of a stand mixer fitted with the paddle attachment, beat the butter, sugar and almond extract on medium speed for 3 to 4 minutes, or until light and fluffy. Scrape the bottom and sides of the bowl as needed. On low speed, slowly mix the dry ingredients into the wet.

Scoop 1 tablespoon (15 g) of the cookie dough and roll it into a smooth ball using your hands. The dough should easily hold a ball shape, but if not, chill it in the fridge for 30 minutes. Repeat with the remaining dough, placing the balls on the baking sheets 2 inches (5 cm) apart. Slightly flatten the dough balls with the palm of your hand or the bottom of a measuring cup. Bake the cookies for 8 to 10 minutes, or until the edges are set and very lightly golden brown. Keep the cookies on the hot baking sheets for 5 minutes before transferring them to a cooling rack to cool to room temperature.

While the cookies cool, make the glaze. In a medium mixing bowl, mix together the confectioners' sugar, almond extract and water and mix until well combined. Stir in 1 additional teaspoon of the water at a time until it is your desired consistency. Spoon the glaze on top of the cooled cookies. Top the wet glaze with the sliced almonds, and allow 30 to 45 minutes for the glaze to fully set before serving.

no-bake cornflake

makes 28 cookies

These cookies are as easy to make as Rice Krispie treats and dare I say, taste even better. They are made from pantry basics and come together in less than 10 minutes. The cornflakes provide a chewy, slightly crispy structure for the cookie, while the creamy peanut butter, honey, cinnamon and marshmallow crème provide sweet, savory and creamy flavors and textures.

INGREDIENTS

1 cup (200 g) granulated sugar

1 cup (240 ml) honey

1 cup (256 g) creamy peanut butter

2 tsp (6 g) ground cinnamon

1 tsp vanilla extract

6 cups (164 g) cornflakes

4 oz (113 g) marshmallow crème

DIRECTIONS

Line a large baking sheet with parchment paper.

In a medium pot, bring the sugar, honey and peanut butter to a boil over medium heat. Stir a couple of times once the sugar begins to melt. Once the mixture begins to boil, remove the pot from the heat. Quickly stir in the cinnamon, vanilla and cornflakes until fully coated and well combined.

The marshmallow crème will be incorporated into the cornflake mixture in two batches. First, drop heaping tablespoons of marshmallow crème onto the cornflake mixture until you've used half of the crème. Gently swirl it in. Do not fully mix. Scoop 2-tablespoon (30-g) amounts of the cookie dough onto the baking sheet until you've used half of the cornflake mixture. Swirl the remaining marshmallow crème into the remaining cornflake mixture and scoop it onto the baking sheet. Allow 30 minutes for the cookies to fully set before serving.

Herbs
bright citrus and woodsy essence

This chapter is perhaps my favorite. While I love ground spices, there is something beautifully wild and innate in baking with fresh herbs and citrus fruits. These flavor pairings are as natural as the moon giving way to the sun each morning. From zesting a lemon and being greeted by a burst of fresh aromatics to running your fingers over rosemary leaves to release its nuanced scents, baking with fresh herbs and citrus is a full sensory experience—one that calls for us to simply let nature lead the way.

Bright is the easiest and most descriptive word I use when referring to citrus. I have a deep love of any and all things lemon. For that reason, you will find many recipes in this chapter that highlight lemon as the main flavor or use it to add a hint of brightness. *Woodsy essence* refers to aromatics of the group of herbs found in the mint family. This family is made from herbs that have highly fragrant leaves and flowers, including lavender, rosemary and thyme, which are perfect for cooking and baking. Lavender has a distinctly floral scent with notes of mint and rosemary. Rosemary is very aromatic with strong notes of pine and mint. Thyme is a beautiful combination of earthy, minty, citrus and savory notes, but it is also sweet. All these herbs pair beautifully with fresh citrus such as lemon, lime and orange. They are made for one another.

There's much to be said for fully appreciating nature's natural pairings. I adore pulling out the contrasts and finding a balance of sweet and savory, floral and citrus. The recipes in this chapter such as the Lemon Thyme Cookie Bars (page 107), Lavender Brownie Cookies (page 108) and Blood Orange Rosemary cookies (page 121) are meant to connect you to your more romantic and whimsical side.

lemon thyme cookie bars

makes 1 (9" [23-cm]) cookie

Lemon has to be my absolute favorite citrus flavor. I'm known to put lemon on just about anything. The fresh tartness that lemons bring to any dish, but especially baked sweets, is spectacular. These cookie bars are thick, chewy, buttery and full of fresh, tart lemon flavor. The hint of thyme brings the slightest bit of savory to balance out the sweet and sour flavors, while the honey lemon glaze adds a subtle floral note that beautifully rounds out the cookie bars.

INGREDIENTS

for the lemon thyme cookie bars

1 cup (200 g) granulated sugar

1 tbsp (2 g) finely chopped fresh thyme leaves (see tip)

Zest of 2 lemons

1 cup (226 g) unsalted butter, room temperature

1 large egg yolk, room temperature

2 cups (240 g) all-purpose flour

¼ cup (28 g) almond flour

½ tsp salt

for the honey lemon glaze

1 cup (120 g) confectioners' sugar

1 tbsp (15 ml) honey

1 tbsp (15 ml) fresh lemon juice, plus more as needed

DIRECTIONS

Preheat the oven to 350°F (180°C). Lightly grease the bottom and sides of a 9-inch (23-cm) springform pan, and line the bottom with parchment paper.

To make the cookie bars, in the bowl of a stand mixer fitted with the paddle attachment, add the sugar, thyme and lemon zest. Mix on low speed until the texture resembles wet sand. On medium speed, beat in the butter for 3 to 4 minutes, or until light and fluffy. Scrape the bottom and sides of the bowl as needed. Mix in the egg yolk until smooth and well combined. On low speed, mix in the flour, almond flour and salt until just combined. If needed, use a spatula or your hands to work any stray bits into the dough.

Evenly press the dough into the prepared pan. Bake for 20 to 25 minutes, or until the edges are set and lightly golden brown and the top is a very lightly toasted color. Cool the cookie in the pan for 20 minutes. Remove the ring of the springform pan, and slice the cookie into wedges. Place the ring back onto the pan.

To make the glaze, in a medium mixing bowl, mix together the confectioners' sugar, honey and lemon juice until pourable and well combined. Add up to 1 additional tablespoon (15 ml) of lemon juice if necessary. Evenly pour the glaze on top of the sliced cookie bars inside the pan. Let the glaze set for 30 to 45 minutes. Remove the ring from the springform pan, slice the cookie bars along the precut lines and enjoy!

tip: You can use 1 teaspoon of dried thyme in place of the fresh thyme, if needed.

lavender brownie cookies

makes 12 large cookies

These cookies have all the best features of a fudge brownie in cookie form. A soft, fudge-like interior meets a glossy, crinkled, paper-thin exterior. The quick and easy lavender sugar provides a lovely and subtle floral note that beautifully complements the sweet citrus of the chocolate.

INGREDIENTS

for the lavender sugar

1½ tsp (1 g) culinary-grade lavender buds

1 cup (200 g) granulated sugar

for the lavender brownie cookies

½ cup (113 g) cubed unsalted butter

8 oz (226 g) good-quality dark (70% or higher cocoa content) chocolate bar, chopped

2 large eggs, room temperature

¼ cup (24 g) Dutch process cocoa powder

2 tsp (6 g) instant espresso powder

1 tsp baking powder

½ tsp salt

¾ cup (90 g) all-purpose flour

Confectioners' sugar, for topping (optional)

DIRECTIONS

Preheat the oven to 350°F (180°C). Line two large baking sheets with parchment paper.

To make the lavender sugar, pulse the lavender buds in a food processor for 5 seconds. Add the sugar and process for 30 seconds. Pour into a small bowl and set aside.

To make the cookies, place the butter and chopped chocolate in a microwave-safe bowl, and heat in the microwave for 1 minute. Carefully pull out the bowl. Stir the melted butter and partially melted chocolate until they are well combined. Heat in 20-second increments, stirring until the butter and chocolate are fully melted and well combined. In a stand mixer fitted with the whisk attachment, whisk together the lavender sugar and eggs on medium speed for 4 to 5 minutes, or until light, fluffy and pale yellow. On low, slowly stream in the chocolate mixture, and beat until well combined. Scrape the bottom and sides of the bowl as needed. Sift in the cocoa powder, espresso powder, baking powder and salt. Whisk on low until smooth and well combined. Scrape the bottom and sides of the bowl as needed. Sift in the flour. Whisk on low, scraping the bowl as needed, until the flour is fully incorporated.

Scoop 3-tablespoon (45-g) amounts of the brownie cookie dough onto the baking sheets, spacing them 2 inches (5 cm) apart. Try to scoop all the cookie dough onto the baking sheets to bake at the same time (see tip). Bake on the center rack for 10 to 14 minutes, or until the edges are fully set and the centers are cracked and barely set. Cool the cookies on the baking sheet placed on top of a cooling rack until fully cooled. Dust lightly with the confectioners' sugar, if you like.

tip: It is important to bake the brownie cookie dough as soon as the dough is mixed. This gives the cookies their glossy tops. If you need to bake the cookies in batches, the second batch will have duller tops.

citrus fennel shortbread bars

makes 1 (8 x 8" [20 x 20-cm]) pan

On its own, fennel tastes a bit like licorice. However, once fennel seeds are ground into a powder and baked into a dish, it imparts a light, bright, spring-like flavor. In other words, it pairs exceptionally well with citrus, which in turn pairs beautifully with butter and sugar. These bars have a soft, melt-in-your-mouth texture that crumbles ever so slightly with each bite. These are the perfect, not-too-sweet, buttery, oh-so-very-delicious cookie bars.

INGREDIENTS

¾ cup (150 g) granulated sugar

Zest of 3 medium lemons or oranges (or a mix)

½ tsp salt

1 cup (226 g) unsalted butter, room temperature

2 tsp (3 g) ground fennel

1 tsp vanilla extract

1 tsp lemon extract

2 cups (240 g) all-purpose flour

DIRECTIONS

Preheat the oven to 350°F (180°C). Line an 8 x 8–inch (20 x 20–cm) aluminum pan with parchment paper, leaving an overhang of 1 to 2 inches (2.5 to 5 cm) on two sides to allow for easy removal.

In the bowl of a stand mixer fitted with the paddle attachment, add the sugar, zest and salt. On low speed, mix until the texture resembles wet sand. Scoop out 1 tablespoon (13 g) of the citrus sugar into a small bowl to use for topping the bars. Set aside.

Add the butter, fennel, vanilla and lemon extract to the citrus sugar in the stand mixer bowl. Cream on low-medium speed for 2 to 3 minutes, or until well combined. Scrape the bottom and sides of the bowl as needed. On low, mix in the flour in two separate batches. Scrape the bottom and sides of the bowl in between each flour addition to help incorporate any stray pieces. Mix the flour until just combined.

Scoop even-sized pieces of the cookie dough into the prepared pan. Press the dough into the corners and across the pan in an even layer. Prick the dough with a fork. Scatter the reserved citrus sugar on top. Bake on the center rack for 25 to 30 minutes, or until the edges are lightly browned and pulled slightly from the edges of the pan. Cool in the pan on top of a cooling rack for 30 to 45 minutes, or until it has cooled completely to room temperature. Using the overhanging parchment paper, gently lift the shortbread out of the pan. Cut into your desired number of pieces and enjoy.

rosemary oatmeal chocolate chip

makes 30 cookies

Cozy and classic meets fresh and vibrant in these cookies. They have the same taste and texture of traditional oatmeal chocolate chip cookies you know and love, but now with notes of citrus and pine. The addition of the rosemary and lemon zest brings a subtle hint of brightness that complements the chocolate chips beautifully. It's a fresh spin on a classic I think you'll absolutely love.

INGREDIENTS

1½ cups (180 g) all-purpose flour

1 tsp baking soda

½ tsp salt

1 cup (200 g) light brown sugar

½ cup (100 g) granulated sugar

1–2 tsp (1–2 g) finely chopped rosemary

Zest of 1 lemon

1 cup (226 g) unsalted butter, room temperature

1 large egg, room temperature

1 large egg yolk, room temperature

2 tsp (10 ml) vanilla extract

2 cups (180 g) rolled oats

1½ cups (255 g) semisweet or milk chocolate chips

DIRECTIONS

In a medium mixing bowl, whisk together the flour, baking soda and salt until well combined. In the bowl of a stand mixer fitted with the paddle attachment, mix the sugars, rosemary and zest on low speed until the texture resembles wet sand. Add the butter and beat on medium speed for 3 minutes, or until well combined. On low, mix in the egg, egg yolk and vanilla until smooth and well combined. Scrape the bottom and sides of the bowl as needed. With the mixer on low, mix the dry ingredients into the wet until just combined. Stir in the oats and chocolate chips. Wrap the dough in plastic wrap, and chill it in the fridge for at least 2 hours and up to overnight.

Preheat the oven to 350°F (180°C). Line a large baking sheet with parchment paper. Pull the cookie dough from the fridge to sit out at room temperature for 20 minutes before baking.

Scoop 2-tablespoon (30-g) amounts of the cookie dough onto the baking sheet 3 inches (8 cm) apart. Bake for 12 to 14 minutes, or until the edges are set. Keep the cookies on the hot baking sheet for 10 minutes before transferring them to a cooling rack to cool to room temperature.

fresh mint chocolate sandwich cookies

makes 16–17 sandwich cookies

Mint and chocolate are such a classic and refreshing pairing. No cookie book would be complete without at least one mint chocolate cookie. These sandwich cookies take that classic pairing and turn them into the cutest, most refreshingly delicious little cookies you could ask for. They are flavored with sweet and spicy cinnamon, while the fresh mint buttercream is infused with both fresh mint and mint extract. The result is a little sandwich cookie that looks and tastes just like mint Oreos . . . but better.

INGREDIENTS

for the mint chocolate cookies

1¾ cups (210 g) all-purpose flour, plus more as needed

2 tsp (6 g) ground cinnamon

1 tsp cornstarch

½ tsp baking powder

½ tsp salt

¾ cup (170 g) unsalted butter, room temperature

¾ cup (150 g) granulated sugar

1 tsp instant espresso powder

½ cup (48 g) Dutch process cocoa powder

1 large egg, room temperature

DIRECTIONS

To make the cookies, in a medium mixing bowl, whisk together the flour, cinnamon, cornstarch, baking powder and salt until well combined. In the bowl of a stand mixer fitted with the paddle attachment, cream the butter, sugar and espresso powder on medium speed for 3 minutes or until well combined. Scrape the bottom and sides of the bowl as needed. On low, cream in the cocoa powder until smooth and well combined. Scrape the bottom and sides of the bowl as needed.

Mix in the egg until smooth and well combined. With the mixer on low, mix the dry ingredients into the wet until just combined. If the dough feels too sticky, mix in 2 to 3 tablespoons (15 to 23 g) of additional flour until the dough feels tacky.

Divide the dough into two equal pieces. Set one piece in the mixing bowl. Drop the second piece onto a large piece of parchment paper, and place a large piece of plastic wrap over it. Roll out the dough to a ¼-inch (6-mm)-thick "sheet." Fully wrap the dough in the plastic wrap. Repeat for the remaining dough ball. Place both "sheets" in the fridge to chill for at least 2 hours and up to overnight.

(continued)

fresh mint chocolate sandwich cookies (continued)

for the fresh mint buttercream

20 fresh mint leaves, roughly torn or chopped

½ cup (113 g) unsalted butter, room temperature

2 cups (240 g) sifted confectioners' sugar

1 tbsp (15 ml) milk, plus more as needed

1 tsp vanilla extract

¼ tsp salt

½ tsp mint extract (optional)

Preheat the oven to 350°F (180°C). Line two large baking sheets with parchment paper.

Remove one sheet of chilled dough. Unwrap the dough and place it onto a piece of parchment paper. Using a small 2-inch (5-cm) biscuit or cookie cutter, cut out rounds of chilled dough. Gently lift the cut pieces onto the baking sheets. Space the cookies 2 inches (5 cm) apart. They shouldn't spread too much while baking. Bake for 9 to 11 minutes, or until set. Keep the cookies on the hot baking sheets for 3 minutes before transferring them to a cooling rack to cool to room temperature. While the first batch of cookies bakes, pull out the second dough sheet and repeat the process. For any excess dough, gently gather the excess dough, roll it back into a ball in plastic wrap, chill it in the fridge until it can hold its shape, and then roll out and cut again; repeat until all the dough is used up.

While the cookies cool, make the fresh mint buttercream. In the bowl of a stand mixer fitted with the paddle attachment, add the mint leaves. Turn the mixer on low to "muddle" the mint. Add the butter and mix on low until smooth and well combined. Mix in the confectioners' sugar ½ cup (60 g) at a time. Mix in the milk, vanilla and salt. Mix on low until all the ingredients are smooth and well combined. If you would like more mint flavor, add the mint extract. If the buttercream is too thick, add 1 teaspoon more milk at a time, up to 2 tablespoons (30 ml), or until the buttercream reaches your desired consistency.

To assemble, apply your desired amount of frosting to the bottom of one cookie. Place the bottom of another cookie on the frosting side of the first cookie and gently press together. Enjoy!

soft lemon cardamom

makes 22 cookies

These cookies are exactly as their name describes! They are pillowy, buttery and packed full of lemon flavor. Enjoy these plain for a simple, not-too-sweet morning treat that pairs nicely with tea or coffee, or top them with the sweet and tangy lemon cream cheese frosting for the ultimate lemon delight.

INGREDIENTS

for the soft lemon cardamom cookies

2 cups (240 g) cake flour

¾ cup (90 g) all-purpose flour

¾ tsp ground cardamom (see tip)

1 tsp baking soda

½ tsp baking powder

½ tsp cream of tartar

¼ tsp salt

¾ cup (150 g) granulated sugar

Zest of 2 lemons

½ cup (113 g) unsalted butter, room temperature

¾ cup (90 g) confectioners' sugar

1 large egg, room temperature

1 tsp lemon extract

1 tsp vanilla extract

½ cup (120 ml) sour cream, room temperature

DIRECTIONS

In a medium mixing bowl, whisk together the cake flour, all-purpose flour, cardamom, baking soda, baking powder, cream of tartar and salt until well combined. In the bowl of a stand mixer fitted with the paddle attachment, mix the granulated sugar and zest on low speed until the texture resembles wet sand. Add the butter and confectioners' sugar and cream on medium speed for 3 to 4 minutes, or until light and fluffy. Scrape the bottom and sides of the bowl as needed. One at a time, mix in the egg, lemon extract, vanilla and sour cream until smooth and well combined. On low speed, mix the dry ingredients into the wet until just combined. Cover the dough with plastic wrap and chill it in the fridge for at least 2 hours and up to overnight.

Preheat the oven to 375°F (190°C). Line two large baking sheets with parchment paper.

Scoop 2-tablespoon (30-g) amounts of cookie dough onto the baking sheets, spacing them 2 inches (5 cm) apart. Slightly flatten each cookie with the palm of your hand or the back of a measuring cup. Bake for 8 to 9 minutes, or until the edges are set and a finger lightly pressed into the center of the cookie bounces back. The cookies will still be light in color. Keep the cookies on the hot baking sheets for 5 minutes before transferring them to a cooling rack to cool to room temperature.

(continued)

soft lemon cardamom (continued)

for the lemon cream cheese frosting

½ cup (113 g) unsalted butter, room temperature

4 oz (113 g) cream cheese, room temperature

2½ cups (300 g) sifted confectioners' sugar, divided

2 tbsp (30 ml) lemon juice

1 tsp vanilla extract

¼ tsp salt

Zest of 1 lemon, for topping (optional)

While the cookies cool, make the lemon cream cheese frosting. In the bowl of a stand mixer fitted with the paddle attachment, cream the butter and cream cheese for 4 to 5 minutes, or until creamy and well combined. Scrape the bottom and sides of the bowl as needed. On low, beat in 1 cup (120 g) of the confectioners' sugar, lemon juice, vanilla and salt until smooth and well combined. Scrape the bottom and sides of the bowl as needed. Beat in the remaining confectioners' sugar on medium speed, and then continue beating until the frosting reaches your desired consistency.

To assemble, apply your desired amount of frosting to each cookie with an icing knife, spoon or piping bag fitted with the tip of your choice. If desired, zest the lemon directly over the frosting for a decorative finish. Store frosted cookies in an airtight container in the fridge.

tip: If you prefer to try a different spice, ground cinnamon is a wonderful substitute for the cardamom.

blood orange rosemary

makes 24 cookies

Citrus and rosemary are such a beautiful flavor pairing. There's a reason you'll often find herbs such as rosemary paired with citrus. These soft and pillowy cookies are full of fresh citrus and a touch of cinnamon. While the color of the blood oranges makes these cookies stand out, any citrus fruit works well here. Fun little fact: These cookies are my two little munchkins' favorite cookies in the entire book.

INGREDIENTS

for the blood orange rosemary cookies

2 cups (240 g) all-purpose flour

1½ tsp (7 g) baking powder

1 tsp ground cinnamon

¼ tsp salt

1 cup (200 g) granulated sugar

Zest of 3 blood oranges (¼ cup [24 g])

2–3 tsp (1–2 g) finely chopped fresh rosemary

½ cup (120 ml) olive oil

1 large egg, room temperature

¼ cup (60 ml) buttermilk, room temperature

for the blood orange glaze

1½ cups (180 g) confectioners' sugar

1 tbsp (30 ml) lemon juice

Zest from ½ blood orange (optional)

1–3 tbsp (15–45 ml) freshly squeezed blood orange juice

DIRECTIONS

To make the cookies, in a medium mixing bowl, whisk together the flour, baking powder, cinnamon and salt until well combined. In a large mixing bowl, whisk the sugar, zest and rosemary until it has the consistency of wet sand. Whisk in the olive oil and egg until smooth and well combined. Alternate mixing the dry ingredients and buttermilk into the wet until all the dry ingredients and buttermilk have been added. Rest the cookie dough at room temperature for 30 minutes.

Preheat the oven to 375°F (190°C). Line two large baking sheets with parchment paper.

Scoop 1-tablespoon (15-g) amounts of cookie dough onto the baking sheets, spacing them 2 inches (5 cm) apart. Bake for 9 to 11 minutes, or until a finger lightly pressed into the top of the cookie bounces back. Keep the cookies on the hot baking sheets for 3 to 4 minutes before transferring them to a cooling rack to cool to room temperature.

While the cookies cool, make the glaze. In a medium mixing bowl, add the confectioners' sugar. Whisk in the lemon juice, zest if using and 1 to 3 tablespoons (15 to 45 ml) of the blood orange juice, to taste. Spoon the glaze over the cooled cookies, and let it set for 30 to 45 minutes before serving.

lemon and lavender pistachio

makes 32–36 cookies

Lemon and lavender are my favorite springtime flavor pairing. This combination of flavors is bright, fresh and floral. Raw pistachios have a mild, sweet, earthy creaminess that makes them an excellent choice to pair with both lavender and lemon. These cookies are soft, chewy, buttery and tart little bites of spring.

INGREDIENTS

for the lemon and lavender pistachio cookies

1 cup (120 g) raw, shelled pistachios

1 tsp culinary-grade lavender buds

1 cup (200 g) granulated sugar

Zest of 2 lemons

1 tsp vanilla extract

1 tsp lemon extract

½ cup (113 g) unsalted butter, room temperature

1 large egg, room temperature

½ tsp salt

1¾ cups (210 g) all-purpose flour

for the lemon glaze

1 cup (120 g) sifted confectioners' sugar

2–3 tbsp (30–45 ml) fresh lemon juice

¼ cup (30 g) finely chopped raw pistachios, for topping

¼ tsp finely chopped culinary-grade lavender buds, for topping

DIRECTIONS

Place the pistachios into a food processor. Process until they resemble coarse sand. Pour into a small bowl and set aside. Place the lavender buds in the food processor. Pulse for 5 seconds. Add the sugar and process for 30 seconds. Add the lavender sugar, zest, vanilla and lemon extract to the bowl of a stand mixer fitted with the paddle attachment. Mix on low speed until the texture resembles wet sand. Cream in the butter on medium speed for 3 minutes, or until well combined. With the mixer on low, mix in the ground pistachios until smooth and well combined. On low, mix in the egg, salt and flour, one at a time, until each is well combined.

Divide the dough into two equal pieces. Set one piece back in the stand mixer bowl. Drop the second piece of dough onto a large piece of parchment paper, and place a large piece of plastic wrap over it. Roll out the dough to a ¼-inch (6-mm)-thick "sheet." Fully wrap the dough in the plastic wrap. Repeat for the remaining dough ball. Place the cookie dough sheets in the fridge to chill for at least 2 hours and up to overnight.

Preheat the oven to 350°F (180°C). Line two large baking sheets with parchment paper. Remove one sheet of chilled dough, and using a small 2-inch (5-cm) biscuit or cookie cutter, cut out rounds of chilled dough and place them on the baking sheets 2 inches (5 cm) apart. Bake 9 to 11 minutes, or until the edges turn a very light golden brown and the centers are lighter in color. Keep the cookies on the hot baking sheets for 3 minutes before transferring them to a cooling rack to cool to room temperature. Repeat the process with the remaining dough.

Make the lemon glaze while the cookies cool. In a medium mixing bowl, mix the confectioners' sugar and lemon juice until the glaze is your desired consistency. Spoon 1 to 2 teaspoons (5 to 10 ml) of glaze on top of each cookie. In a small mixing bowl, mix together the pistachios and lavender buds. Sprinkle on top of the glaze after it has set for 5 minutes. The glaze will be fully set after 30 to 45 minutes.

orange macadamia nut

makes 24 cookies

Macadamia nuts are sweet, buttery and creamy nuts that grow in tropical climates. Playing off this flavor profile, I wanted to use sweet, bright spices such as cinnamon, cardamom and orange to complement the natural tropical flavors of the nut. The addition of the white chocolate is a traditional pairing and brings another layer of rich creaminess to the cookies. In short, these cookies are incredibly delicious!

INGREDIENTS

for the orange macadamia nut cookies

1 cup (128 g) macadamia nuts

1¾ cups (210 g) all-purpose flour

1 tsp ground cardamom

1 tsp ground cinnamon

½ tsp ground cloves

½ tsp baking powder

¼ tsp baking soda

½ tsp salt

1 cup (200 g) light brown sugar

½ cup (100 g) granulated sugar

Zest of 1 medium orange

½ cup (113 g) unsalted butter, room temperature

2 large eggs, room temperature

1 tsp vanilla extract

12 oz (340 g) white chocolate, evenly chopped

for the citrus sugar

½ cup (100 g) granulated sugar

Zest of 1 medium orange

¼ tsp salt

DIRECTIONS

To make the cookies, place the macadamia nuts into a food processor, and process until they resemble coarse sand or the texture of almond flour. This takes several pulses. Pour into a small bowl and set aside. In a medium mixing bowl, whisk together the flour, cardamom, cinnamon, cloves, baking powder, baking soda and salt until well combined. In the bowl of a stand mixer fitted with the paddle attachment, mix the sugars and zest on low speed until the texture resembles wet sand. Beat in the butter and orange sugar on medium speed for 3 to 4 minutes, or until light and fluffy. Scrape the bottom and sides of the bowl as needed. One at a time, beat in the ground macadamia nuts, eggs and vanilla until smooth and well combined. On low speed, stir the dry ingredients into the wet until just combined. Fold in the white chocolate. Cover the dough with plastic wrap and chill it in the fridge for at least 2 hours. The cookies can be stored this way for up to 2 days.

Make the citrus sugar by placing the sugar, zest and salt in a wide, shallow bowl, mixing until the mixture resembles wet sand.

Preheat the oven to 375°F (190°C). Line two large baking sheets with parchment paper.

Scoop 2-tablespoon (30-g) amounts of the cookie dough and roll the dough into balls with your hands. Roll each ball in the citrus sugar, and place them on the parchment-lined baking sheets 3 inches (8 cm) apart. Bake for 11 to 14 minutes, or until the edges of the cookies are golden brown and set. Keep the cookies on the hot baking sheet for 5 minutes before transferring them to a cooling rack to cool to room temperature.

mint lime shortbread

makes 30 cookies

These bite-size shortbread cookies are rich, soft and slightly crumbly with just a hint of vibrant lime and cool mint. The fresh lime glaze provides a deliciously tart and tangy brightness that pairs perfectly with the buttery base. If summer was a cookie, it would be these cookies!

INGREDIENTS

for the mint lime shortbread cookies

¾ cup (150 g) granulated sugar

Zest of 2–3 limes (1½ tbsp [9 g])

¼ cup (6 g) finely chopped mint leaves (about 20 mint leaves)

1 cup (226 g) unsalted butter, room temperature

2 cups (240 g) all-purpose flour

½ cup (56 g) almond flour

¼ tsp salt

for the lime glaze

2–3 tbsp (30–45 ml) fresh lime juice (from 2 limes)

1 cup (120 g) confectioners' sugar

Zest of 1 lime, for topping (optional)

DIRECTIONS

To make the cookies, in the bowl of a stand mixer fitted with the paddle attachment, add the sugar, zest and mint leaves. On low speed, mix until the texture resembles wet sand and is very fragrant. On medium speed, beat in the butter for 3 to 4 minutes, or until light and fluffy. Scrape the bottom and sides of the bowl as needed. On low speed, mix in the flour, almond flour and salt until well combined. Scrape the bottom and sides of the bowl as needed. Mix on low for 30 seconds to incorporate any stray pieces of dough. Wrap the dough in plastic wrap, and chill it in the fridge for 30 minutes.

Preheat the oven to 350°F (180°C). Line two large baking sheets with parchment paper.

Scoop 1-tablespoon (15-g) amounts of the cookie dough onto the baking sheets, spacing them 2 inches (5 cm) apart. Bake for 12 to 14 minutes, or until the edges are lightly golden brown. Keep the cookies on the hot baking sheet for 3 to 4 minutes before transferring them to a cooling rack to cool to room temperature.

While the cookies cool, make the lime glaze. In a small mixing bowl, whisk together the lime juice and confectioners' sugar until smooth and well combined. Spoon the glaze on top of the cookies, and allow it to set for 5 minutes before topping with the lime zest, if using. Let the glaze set for 20 to 25 minutes before serving.

no-bake mint chocolate

makes 22 cookies

The inspiration for these cookies comes from everyone's favorite classic, thin mints. (I'm not the only one who devours a whole sleeve in one sitting, right?) One of my favorite ways to enjoy thin mints is straight from the fridge with a generous dollop of peanut butter on top. These are like a cross between thin mints topped with peanut butter and oatmeal cookies. The oatmeal provides structure and a wholesome texture. The peanut butter and chocolate are the dominant flavors, while the mint provides a refreshingly cool background flavor.

INGREDIENTS

½ cup (113 g) unsalted butter

1½ cups (300 g) granulated sugar

½ cup (120 ml) milk

¼ cup (24 g) unsweetened or Dutch process cocoa powder

4 sprigs mint leaves with 20–30 leaves

1 cup (256 g) creamy peanut butter

2 tsp (10 ml) vanilla extract

2¾ cups (248 g) rolled oats

1 tsp mint or peppermint extract (optional)

DIRECTIONS

In a small saucepan, heat the butter, sugar, milk, cocoa powder and mint over medium heat, whisking continually until the butter has fully melted. Bring the mixture to a boil. Boil for 1 minute, and then pour the mixture through a mesh strainer into a large mixing bowl. Discard the mint leaves and stems caught in the strainer. Stir in the peanut butter and vanilla until smooth and well combined. Stir in the oats until well combined. Taste the mixture. If you would like a more pronounced mint taste, add up to 1 teaspoon of mint or peppermint extract. Allow the cookie mixture to sit at room temperature for 10 minutes to thicken slightly.

Line two large baking sheets with parchment paper.

Scoop 2-tablespoon (30-g) amounts of the mixture onto the baking sheets, spacing them 2 inches (5 cm) apart. Place the cookies in the fridge for 1 hour to fully set before serving. These should be stored in an airtight container in the fridge.

Fruit
fresh and floral

In much the same way as baking with fresh herbs and citrus is a feast for the senses, so too is baking with fresh fruits. Simply preparing the fruit for the recipe awakens and engages your senses in a totally unique way. Selecting the perfect fruit for the recipe, as well as washing, drying and tasting that fruit are all part of the baking process, before you even turn on the oven. In this chapter, you will find recipes that utilize the natural flavors of fruit while enhancing that flavor with spices.

Fresh and *floral* are the first words that come to mind when I enjoy a fresh summer berry or crisp apple come fall. The fruits and spices that form the flavor profiles in this chapter are based around the idea of embracing and enhancing the beauty that is baking with fruit in the peak of its ripeness.

Lemon and cardamom bring bright and tart back notes to raspberries as found in the Raspberry Cardamom bakery-style cookies (page 133). Lemon, cardamom and rosewater work beautifully in complementing the tangy cream cheese and fresh berries that fill the Berry-Filled Lemon Sugar Cookie Cups (page 141). One spice that you may find a bit odd is the use of coriander. When used in small amounts, coriander actually accentuates the full flavor of berries, and blueberries in particular, while remaining undetectable as a stand-alone flavor. For something with a little more spice, the Mixed Berry Skillet Cookie (page 134) and the Maple-Glazed Apple Cookies (page 157) are full of sweet and spicy flavors.

raspberry cardamom

makes 8 cookies

Of all the cookies in this chapter, these bakery-style cookies are my absolute favorite. They are the perfect combination of toasted exterior and soft, cake-like interior. They are sweet and buttery, with pops of tart raspberry and pockets of melted white chocolate all complemented by a hint of bright cardamom. They are easy to make, yet look like they came straight from the local bakery.

INGREDIENTS

1¾ cups (210 g) all-purpose flour

2 tbsp (20 g) cornstarch

½ tsp baking powder

½ tsp baking soda

1 tsp ground cardamom

½ tsp ground cinnamon

¼ tsp salt

½ cup (113 g) cold unsalted butter, cubed

½ cup (100 g) granulated sugar

¼ cup (50 g) light brown sugar

Zest of 1 lemon

1 large egg, room temperature

1 tsp vanilla extract

½ tsp lemon extract

4 oz (113 g) white chocolate, evenly chopped

½ cup (93 g) fresh raspberries, cleaned and dried

DIRECTIONS

Preheat the oven to 375°F (190°C). Line two large baking sheets with parchment paper.

In a medium mixing bowl, whisk together the flour, cornstarch, baking powder, baking soda, cardamom, cinnamon and salt until well combined. In the bowl of a stand mixer fitted with the paddle attachment, beat the butter on medium-high speed for 2 minutes. Scrape the bottom and sides of the bowl as needed. Beat in the sugars on low speed. Once all the sugar has been added, beat on medium speed for 3 minutes, or until light, fluffy and well combined. Scrape the bottom and sides of the bowl as needed. Beat in the zest, egg, vanilla and lemon extract on low until smooth and well combined. Mix the dry ingredients into the wet until just combined. Fold in the white chocolate and gently fold in the fresh raspberries.

Roughly divide the dough into eight equally sized pieces. Form each into a ball. Place four cookie dough balls onto each baking sheet. Bake for 14 to 16 minutes, or until lightly golden and with set edges. They will be very fragrant. Cool the cookies on the hot baking sheet until completely cooled to room temperature and enjoy!

mixed berry skillet cookie

makes 1 (9" [23-cm]) skillet cookie

This recipe captures the best flavors of the warm weather months in an easy-to-make skillet cookie. It's perfect for when you have a bunch of fresh, juicy berries and you want to do a little something extra with them. Think of this skillet cookie as a giant brown-butter chocolate chip cookie with pockets of sweet, tart and jammy berries and a hint of spice throughout.

INGREDIENTS

for the brown butter

½ cup + 2 tbsp (141 g) unsalted butter

for the mixed berry skillet cookie

1¾ cups (210 g) all-purpose flour

1 tsp ground cinnamon

½ tsp ground coriander

½ tsp baking powder

½ tsp baking soda

½ tsp salt

½ cup (100 g) light brown sugar

½ cup (100 g) granulated sugar

Zest of 1 lemon

1 large egg, room temperature

1 tsp vanilla extract

½ cup (85 g) milk or white chocolate chips, divided

1 cup (160 g) mixed fresh berries, cleaned and dried

Vanilla ice cream, for topping

DIRECTIONS

Melt the butter in a heavy bottom saucepan over medium heat for 7 to 10 minutes, or until the butter starts to foam. Whisk continuously until brown bits start to form. Depending on your stove and saucepan, the entire process should take 10 to 15 minutes. Immediately remove the pan from the heat, and pour the brown butter into a clean bowl to cool slightly.

Preheat the oven to 350°F (180°C). Lightly grease a 9-inch (23-cm) cast-iron skillet.

In a medium mixing bowl, whisk together the flour, cinnamon, coriander, baking powder, baking soda and salt until well combined. In a large mixing bowl, add the sugars and zest and whisk together until the sugar resembles the texture of wet sand. Whisk in the slightly cooled brown butter, egg and vanilla until smooth and well combined. Stir the dry ingredients into the wet until just combined. Stir in 6 tablespoons (64 g) of the milk or white chocolate chips.

Evenly spread the cookie dough into the prepared pan. Gently press the fresh berries into the cookie dough. Top with the remaining chocolate chips. Bake for 28 to 35 minutes, or until the edges of the cookie pull away slightly from the edges of the pan. Cool the cookie in the pan placed on a cooling rack for 30 minutes, or until the pan is cool enough to touch. Top with vanilla ice cream right before serving.

strawberry rhubarb cookie bars

makes 1 (8 x 8" [20 x 20-cm]) pan

There's just so much to love in these cookie bars. They are a decadently buttery cookie bar that is chewy on the inside and lightly toasted on the outside. Add in the sweet, tart homemade jam swirled on top and it's pure cookie magic.

INGREDIENTS

for the strawberry rhubarb jam

1 cup (150 g) quartered strawberries

½ cup (65 g) diced rhubarb

½ cup (120 ml) maple syrup

for the spiced cookie bars

1¾ cups (210 g) all-purpose flour

¼ cup (28 g) almond flour

1½ tsp (4 g) ground cinnamon

½ tsp ground nutmeg

¼ tsp ground coriander

½ tsp salt

¾ cup (170 g) unsalted butter, room temperature

1 cup (200 g) granulated sugar

1 large egg, room temperature

1 tsp vanilla extract

DIRECTIONS

To make the jam, in a medium saucepan or skillet, bring the strawberries, rhubarb and maple syrup to a boil over medium heat. Reduce to a simmer and cook for 20 to 25 minutes. The jam should be thick enough to coat the back of a spoon. Cool to room temperature before using in the recipe.

Preheat the oven to 350°F (180°C). Lightly grease the bottom of an 8 x 8–inch (20 x 20–cm) aluminum pan and line it with parchment paper, leaving 1 to 2 inches (2.5 to 5 cm) of an overhang on two sides to allow for easy removal.

To make the cookie bars, in a medium mixing bowl, whisk together the flour, almond flour, cinnamon, nutmeg, coriander and salt. In the bowl of a stand mixer fitted with the paddle attachment, cream the butter and sugar on medium speed for 3 to 4 minutes, or until light and fluffy. Mix in the egg and vanilla until smooth and well combined. Mix the dry ingredients into the wet until just combined.

Evenly press the cookie dough into the prepared pan. Drop dollops of the cooled strawberry rhubarb jam onto the cookie dough and swirl it into the dough with a butter knife. Bake for 28 to 32 minutes, or until the edges of the cookie bars are set and lightly golden and pull slightly from the edges of the pan. Keep the cookie bars in the hot pan for 30 minutes before transferring them to a cooling rack to cool to room temperature. Slice and enjoy!

strawberry cheesecake sugar cookies

makes 16 cookies

These cookies may look like the average sugar cookie, but don't be fooled. They are pure handheld decadence. They have a toasted, crunchy, sugar-coated exterior that contrasts wonderfully with the sweet, creamy strawberry cream cheese—filled interior.

INGREDIENTS

for the strawberry cheesecake filling

6 oz (170 g) cream cheese, softened

3 tbsp (38 g) granulated sugar

½ tsp vanilla extract

¼ tsp ground cinnamon

¼ tsp salt

¼ cup (60 ml) strawberry preserves

for the spiced sugar cookies

2½ cups (300 g) all-purpose flour

1 tsp cornstarch

2 tsp (9 g) baking powder

2 tsp (6 g) ground cinnamon

¼ tsp salt

1 cup (200 g) granulated sugar

¼ cup (50 g) light brown sugar

Zest of 2 lemons

¾ cup (170 g) unsalted butter, room temperature

1 large egg, room temperature

1 large egg yolk, room temperature

1 tsp vanilla extract

1 tsp lemon extract

DIRECTIONS

To make the filling, in a medium mixing bowl, mix together the cream cheese, sugar, vanilla, cinnamon and salt until smooth and well combined. Swirl in the strawberry preserves. Cover the bowl with plastic wrap and freeze until ready to use in the recipe.

To make the cookies, in a medium mixing bowl, whisk together the flour, cornstarch, baking powder, cinnamon and salt until well combined. In the bowl of a stand mixer fitted with the paddle attachment, mix the sugars and zest on low until the sugar starts to feel like wet sand. Beat in the butter for 3 to 4 minutes, or until light, fluffy and well combined. Scrape the bottom and sides of the bowl as needed. On low, beat in the egg, egg yolk, vanilla and lemon extract. Mix the dry ingredients into the wet until just combined. Scrape the bottom and sides of the bowl as needed. Cover the dough with plastic wrap and chill it in the fridge for 30 to 45 minutes, or until the dough easily holds a ball shape.

(continued)

for the spiced sugar

¼ cup (50 g) granulated sugar

1 tsp ground cinnamon

To make the spiced sugar, in a wide, shallow bowl, whisk the sugar and cinnamon until well combined.

Line a small baking sheet or large plate with parchment paper. Remove the sugar cookie dough from the fridge and the cream cheese mixture from the freezer. Scoop 1 tablespoon (15 g) of the cookie dough, flatten it in your hand and place it onto the lined baking sheet or plate. Using a teaspoon, scoop the filling into the center of the flattened cookie dough. Scoop another cookie dough ball and flatten. Place the second flattened cookie dough on top of the cookie dough with the filling. Press the edges together, creating a seal. Gently roll the filled cookie dough into a ball. Press any cracks in the dough back together. Roll in the spiced sugar, and then place back onto the lined baking sheet or plate. Repeat for all the remaining dough and filling. Place the prepared cookie balls in the freezer for 30 minutes.

Preheat the oven to 375°F (190°C). Line two large baking sheets with parchment paper.

Place the dough balls on the baking sheets 3 inches (8 cm) apart. If you have to bake in batches, leave the remaining dough balls in the freezer until ready to bake. Bake the cookies for 12 to 14 minutes, or until the edges of the cookies are set and a light golden brown color. The tops of the cookies may show small cracks. Keep the cookies on the hot baking sheet for 5 minutes before transferring them to a cooling rack to cool to room temperature. Store the cookies in an airtight container in the fridge.

berry-filled lemon sugar cookie cups

makes 16 large or 32 mini cups

The inspiration for these cookie cups comes from fruit pizza. While I was growing up, there always seemed to be a fruit pizza on the dessert table at every family gathering in the summer. For those who don't know, fruit pizza is basically a giant sugar cookie topped with a sweet and creamy filling and lots of fresh fruit. This recipe takes that same concept and turns it into delicious bite-size cookie cups. Use this recipe as a starting-off point to customize the spices in the cookie, the sweetness of the filling and the fresh toppings. I adore the flavor of rosewater, and it pairs beautifully with the macerated berries in these cookie cups. It does have a very strong floral scent, so if you don't care for floral flavors or don't have it on hand, feel free to use lemon juice.

INGREDIENTS

for the lemon sugar cookie cups

2½ cups (300 g) all-purpose flour

1 tsp ground cinnamon

½ tsp baking soda

½ tsp baking powder

¼ tsp salt

1¼ cups (250 g) granulated sugar

Zest of 2 lemons

1 cup (226 g) unsalted butter, room temperature

1 large egg, room temperature

1 tsp lemon extract

1 tsp vanilla extract

½ tsp rosewater or lemon juice (optional)

DIRECTIONS

Preheat the oven to 350°F (180°C). Lightly grease a 12-count muffin pan or 24-count mini-muffin pan.

To make the cookie cups, in a medium mixing bowl, whisk together the flour, cinnamon, baking soda, baking powder and salt. In the bowl of a stand mixer fitted with the paddle attachment, add the sugar and zest. On low speed, mix until the texture resembles wet sand. On medium speed, beat in the butter for 3 to 4 minutes, or until light and fluffy. Scrape the bottom and sides of the bowl as needed. Mix in the egg, lemon extract, vanilla and rosewater (if using) until smooth and well combined. On low, mix the dry ingredients into the wet until just combined. If needed, use a spatula or your hands to work any stray pieces into the dough.

For a regular muffin pan, scoop 2-tablespoon (30-g) amounts of cookie dough, and for a mini-muffin pan, scoop 1-tablespoon (15-g) amounts of cookie dough, to fill each of the muffin cups. Press the dough up the sides to form a cup shape. Bake for 10 to 14 minutes, or until the edges are set and lightly golden brown. Cool the cookies in the pan for 10 minutes. Use a small measuring spoon or regular spoon to reform the cup shape. To remove the cookies, place a cooling rack on top of the muffin pan. Carefully invert the pan onto the cooling rack. Firmly tap each muffin cup to release the cookie.

(continued)

berry-filled lemon sugar cookie cups (continued)

for the lemon honey cream cheese and berries

2 cups (320 g) mixed fresh berries

2–3 tsp (5–15 g) granulated sugar

¼ tsp rosewater or lemon juice (optional)

8 oz (226 g) cream cheese

½–1 cup (60–120 g) confectioners' sugar

2–3 tbsp (30–45 ml) honey

1 tbsp (15 ml) lemon juice

½ tsp vanilla extract

¼ tsp ground cinnamon

While the cookies cool, make the filling. In a large bowl, gently toss the mixed berries, granulated sugar and rosewater (if using). Allow the berries to sit for 30 to 60 minutes at room temperature. In the bowl of a stand mixer fitted with the paddle attachment, cream together the cream cheese, ½ cup (60 g) of the confectioners' sugar, 2 tablespoons (30 ml) of the honey, lemon juice, vanilla and cinnamon for 3 to 4 minutes, or until creamy and well combined. Scrape the bottom and sides of the bowl as needed. For a sweeter filling, add up to an additional ½ cup (60 g) of confectioners' sugar and/or up to an additional 1 tablespoon (15 ml) of honey.

Using a spoon, 1-tablespoon (15-g)-sized cookie scoop or a piping bag with the piping tip of your choice, apply your desired amount of filling into each cookie cup. Top with the macerated berries and enjoy! Store in an airtight container in the fridge.

lemon blueberry whoopie pies

makes 16 small whoopie pies

Are whoopie pies cookies or small cakes? With this being a cookie book, I'm going with cookies! These are made from soft, pillowy cookies filled with sweet and tart blueberries. They are held together with a cinnamon spice and lemon cream cheese frosting that is beyond delicious when combined with the little cake-like cookies. These whoopie pies are the perfect two-bite cookie.

INGREDIENTS

for the lemon blueberry whoopie pies

2 cups (240 g) all-purpose flour

1½ tsp (7 g) baking powder

¼ tsp coriander

¼ tsp salt

¾ cup (150 g) granulated sugar

Zest of 2 lemons

½ cup (113 g) unsalted butter, room temperature

1 egg, room temperature

1 tsp vanilla extract

1 tsp lemon extract

2 tbsp (30 ml) lemon juice

¼ cup (60 ml) buttermilk, room temperature

1 cup (148 g) fresh blueberries, cleaned and dried

for the spiced lemon frosting

¼ cup (57 g) unsalted butter, room temperature

4 oz (113 g) cream cheese, room temperature

Zest of 1 lemon

1 tsp ground cinnamon

1 tbsp (15 ml) lemon juice

1 tsp vanilla extract

¼ tsp salt

2 cups (240 g) confectioners' sugar, plus more as needed

DIRECTIONS

Preheat the oven to 375°F (190°C). Line two large baking sheets with parchment paper.

In a medium mixing bowl, whisk together the flour, baking powder, coriander and salt until well combined. In the bowl of a stand mixer fitted with the paddle attachment, mix the sugar and zest on low until the sugar starts to feel like wet sand. Beat in the butter for 3 to 4 minutes, or until light, fluffy and well combined. Scrape the bottom and sides of the bowl as needed. Mix in the egg, vanilla, lemon extract and lemon juice until smooth and well combined. On low speed, mix the dry ingredients into the wet, alternating with the buttermilk until just combined. Fold in the blueberries. Scoop 1-tablespoon (15-g) amounts of cookie dough onto the baking sheets, spacing them 2 inches (5 cm) apart. Bake for 9 to 11 minutes, or until the edges are set and a finger lightly pressed into the center of the cookie bounces back. The cookies will still be light in color. Keep the cookies on the hot baking sheets for 3 to 4 minutes before transferring them to a cooling rack to cool to room temperature.

While the cookies cool, make the spiced lemon frosting. In the bowl of a stand mixer fitted with the paddle attachment, cream the butter and cream cheese for 3 to 4 minutes, or until creamy and well combined. Scrape the bottom and sides of the bowl as needed. Add the zest, cinnamon, lemon juice, vanilla and salt, and mix on low until smooth and well combined. Mix in the confectioners' sugar slowly, ½ cup (60 g) at a time. Once fully combined, taste and add more sugar as needed.

To assemble, apply the desired amount of filling to the bottom of one cookie. Place the bottom of another cookie to the frosted side of the first cookie and gently press together. Repeat using all your cookies and frosting.

banana peanut butter cup

makes 18 cookies

This recipe brings together soft and chewy banana-filled cookies with pockets of melted peanut butter cups. Don't let the appearance of these cookies fool you into thinking they are just your average cookie. With each bite, you will taste sweet banana, nutty brown butter, toasted peanut butter and milky chocolate. They are the cookies you never knew you needed in your life, but they will quickly become the ones you make over and over again.

INGREDIENTS

for the brown butter

½ cup + 2 tbsp (141 g) unsalted butter

for the banana peanut butter cup cookies

1½ cups (180 g) all-purpose flour

2 tsp (6 g) ground cinnamon

½ tsp baking soda

½ tsp salt

½ cup (100 g) light brown sugar

¼ cup (50 g) granulated sugar

⅓ cup (126 g) mashed ripe banana (1 large)

1 large egg yolk, room temperature

1½ tsp (8 ml) vanilla extract

1 cup (170 g) mini peanut butter cups or chopped regular-size peanut butter cups

Flaky salt, for topping (optional)

DIRECTIONS

Melt the butter in a heavy bottom saucepan over medium heat for 7 to 10 minutes, or until the butter starts to foam. Whisk continuously until brown bits start to form. Depending on your stove and saucepan, the entire process should take 10 to 15 minutes. Immediately remove the pan from the heat, and pour the brown butter into a large mixing bowl to cool slightly.

In a medium mixing bowl, whisk together the flour, ground cinnamon, baking soda and salt until well combined. In the large mixing bowl with the slightly cooled brown butter, stir in the sugars, banana, egg yolk and vanilla until smooth and well combined. Stir the dry ingredients into the wet until just combined. Stir in the mini peanut butter cups. Cover the dough in plastic wrap, and chill it in the fridge for 2 hours.

Preheat the oven to 350°F (180°C). Line two large baking sheets with parchment paper.

Scoop 2-tablespoon (30-g) amounts of the cookie dough onto the baking sheets, spacing them 3 inches (8 cm) apart. Bake for 10 to 12 minutes, or until the edges are set and lightly golden brown. To get perfectly round-shaped cookies, reshape the cookies using a circular pastry ring slightly larger than the cookies. Swirl the cookie gently around the inside of the ring, nudging the edges into a more circular shape. Sprinkle with the flaky salt, if you like. Keep the cookies on the hot baking sheets for 5 minutes before transferring them to a cooling rack to cool to room temperature.

homemade strawberry pop-tart® cookie bars

makes 1 (8 x 8" [20 x 20–cm]) pan

As a child of the 1990s, Pop-Tarts® were *the* thing to have for breakfast, lunch, snacks . . . anytime really. This recipe started off as a simple shortbread cookie bar with jam in the middle and crumble on top. But through a serendipitous turn of events, it became my giant version of homemade, Pop-Tart-inspired cookie bars. These have a wonderfully buttery shortbread cookie with a layer of strawberry preserves inside. The cookie bars are then topped with a strawberry jam glaze and sprinkles. Think of these as a grown-up version of that iconic childhood treat.

INGREDIENTS

for the strawberry pastry bars

1¾ cups (210 g) all-purpose flour

¾ cup (85 g) almond flour

2 tsp (6 g) ground ginger

½ tsp salt

1 cup (226 g) unsalted butter, room temperature

¾ cup (150 g) granulated sugar

1 large egg, room temperature

1 tsp vanilla extract

1 cup (240 ml) strawberry preserves

DIRECTIONS

Lightly grease the bottom of an 8 x 8–inch (20 x 20–cm) aluminum pan and line it with parchment paper, leaving 1 to 2 inches (2.5 to 5 cm) of an overhang on two sides to allow for easy removal.

To make the bars, in a medium mixing bowl, whisk together the all-purpose flour, almond flour, ground ginger and salt until well combined. In the bowl of a stand mixer fitted with the paddle attachment, beat the butter and sugar on medium speed for 3 to 4 minutes, or until light, fluffy and well combined. Scrape the bottom and sides of the bowl as needed. On low, beat in the egg and vanilla. Mix the dry ingredients into the wet until just combined. If needed, use a spatula or your hands to work any stray pieces into the dough.

Roughly divide the dough into two equal pieces. Press half of the dough into the bottom of the prepared pan. If needed, use a little dough from the second dough ball. Spread the strawberry preserves across the dough. Top the preserves with the remaining dough by taking a scoop of dough, flattening it with your hands and then lightly pressing it onto the preserves. Repeat until all the dough is used. Don't worry about small gaps in the dough; the dough will spread and close as it bakes. Place the uncovered pan in the fridge to chill for 30 minutes.

(continued)

for the strawberry jam glaze

1 cup (120 g) confectioners' sugar

2 tbsp (30 ml) strawberry preserves

1–2 tbsp (15–30 ml) heavy cream

Sprinkles, for topping

Preheat the oven to 350°F (180°C).

Remove the pan from the fridge and place it straight into the oven to bake for 35 to 40 minutes, or until the top is lightly golden brown and the jam bubbles on the sides. The edges of the cookie bars will pull slightly from the pan. Cool the cookies in the pan for 30 minutes. Take a butter knife and gently run it along the unlined sides of the pan to loosen any stuck pieces of baked preserves. Place the entire pan in the fridge for 2 hours to set. When it's time to apply the glaze, carefully remove the bars from the pan using the overhangs.

To make the glaze, in a medium mixing bowl, whisk together the confectioners' sugar, strawberry preserves and 1 tablespoon (15 ml) of the heavy cream until well combined and a thick glaze forms. Add the second tablespoon (15 ml) of heavy cream if needed. Spread the glaze on top of the chilled bars. Top with sprinkles and slice.

spiced vanilla cranberry sandwich cookies

makes 16–17 sandwich cookies

These cute sandwich cookies are full of festive holiday flavor. The spiced vanilla cookie is the perfect blend of texture and flavor contrasts, with a slightly crisp bite complementing the creamy texture of the filling. Warming flavors such as cinnamon, nutmeg and clove provide a spicy balance to the sweet, bright and tart flavor of the cranberry filling.

INGREDIENTS

for the spiced vanilla cookies

1½ cups (180 g) all-purpose flour, plus more as needed

⅓ cup (30 g) almond flour

2 tsp (6 g) ground cinnamon

½ tsp ground nutmeg

¼ tsp ground cloves

¼ tsp baking powder

¼ tsp salt

¾ cup (170 g) unsalted butter, room temperature

½ cup (100 g) granulated sugar

Zest of ½ medium orange

1 large egg, room temperature

1 tsp vanilla extract

for the cranberry puree

2 cups (200 g) fresh or frozen cranberries

3 tbsp (38 g) granulated sugar

Zest of ½ medium orange

2 tbsp (30 ml) freshly squeezed orange juice

DIRECTIONS

To make the cookies, in a medium mixing bowl, sift and whisk the all-purpose flour, almond flour, cinnamon, nutmeg, cloves, baking powder and salt until well combined. In the bowl of a stand mixer fitted with the paddle attachment, beat the butter and sugar on medium speed for 2 to 3 minutes, or until well combined. Scrape the bottom and sides of the bowl as needed. Mix in the zest. Add the egg and vanilla, mixing on low speed for 20 to 30 seconds, or until each is incorporated. Scrape the bottom and sides of the bowl as needed. Beat on medium speed for 30 seconds to fully mix and incorporate everything. Add one half of the dry ingredients into the wet, mixing on the lowest speed until *just* combined. Repeat with the remaining dry ingredients. Scrape the bottom and sides of the bowl as needed. If the dough feels too sticky to handle, add in up to 2 to 3 tablespoons (16 to 24 g) of additional all-purpose flour, 1 tablespoon (8 g) at a time, until the dough feels tacky, but not overly sticky.

Divide the dough into two equal pieces. Set one piece back in the mixing bowl. Drop the second piece onto a large piece of parchment paper. Place a large piece of plastic wrap over the single ball of dough. Roll out the dough to a ¼-inch (6-mm)-thick "sheet." Fully wrap the dough in the plastic wrap. Repeat for the remaining dough ball. Place the cookie dough in the fridge to chill for at least 2 hours and up to overnight.

While the cookie dough chills, make the cranberry puree. Heat the cranberries, sugar, zest and orange juice in a small saucepan or pot over medium-high heat for 4 to 5 minutes, or until the cranberries "pop" and begin to break down into a thick mixture. Remove from the heat to cool slightly. Pour the warm, but not hot, cranberries into a food processor. Process until completely smooth. Place a mesh strainer over a medium mixing bowl. Pour the cranberry puree into the mesh strainer. Press the puree through the strainer for a smoother puree. Cool the puree to room temperature before making the filling.

(continued)

spiced vanilla cranberry sandwich cookies (continued)

for the cranberry filling

¾ cup (170 g) unsalted butter, room temperature

⅓ cup (80 ml) prepared cranberry puree

1 tsp vanilla extract

¼ tsp salt

2½–2¾ cups (300–330 g) sifted confectioners' sugar

1–2 tbsp (15–30 ml) milk (optional)

Preheat the oven to 350°F (180°C). Line two large baking sheets with parchment paper.

Place one dough sheet onto a piece of parchment paper. Using a small 2-inch (5-cm) biscuit or cookie cutter, cut out rounds of chilled dough. Repeat until all the dough has been cut into round pieces. Gently gather the excess dough, and roll it back into a ball in plastic wrap. Chill it in the fridge to be rolled out for another batch. Gently lift the cut pieces of dough onto the baking sheets, spacing them 2 inches (5 cm) apart. Bake for 10 to 12 minutes, or until the edges turn a very light golden brown and the centers are lighter in color. Remove the cookies from the oven. Keep the cookies on the hot baking sheets for 3 minutes before transferring them to a cooling rack to cool to room temperature. While the first batch of cookies bakes, pull out the second dough sheet and repeat the process.

While the cookies cool, make the filling. In the bowl of a stand mixer fitted with the paddle attachment, cream the butter and cranberry puree on medium-low speed for 4 to 5 minutes, or until creamy and well combined. Scrape the bottom and sides of the bowl as needed. Beat in the vanilla and salt on low until smooth and well combined. Add the confectioners' sugar, ½ cup (60 g) at a time, beating each until incorporated. Scrape the bottom and sides of the bowl as needed. Beat on medium until the buttercream is fully incorporated and to your desired consistency. If the buttercream is too thick, add 1 to 2 tablespoons (15 to 30 ml) of milk, beating until well incorporated.

To assemble, apply the desired amount of filling to the bottom of one cookie. Place the bottom of another cookie to the frosted side of the first cookie. Gently press together and repeat. Unfrosted cookies can be stored in an airtight container at room temperature. Once the cookies are sandwiched together, they should be stored individually wrapped in wax paper in an airtight container in the fridge or freezer.

tip: Store the filling in an airtight container in the fridge until ready to apply to the cookies. Bring the filling to room temperature before applying to the cookies.

raspberry snowballs

makes 32 cookies

For this chapter, I really wanted to make a whimsical recipe, and I decided to use Mexican wedding cookies (also called snowball cookies) as my inspiration. This raspberry rendition is sweet, buttery and lightly tart. The addition of the coriander intensifies the flavor of the raspberries. Once baked, the cookies are tossed in a raspberry confectioners' sugar mix that adds another layer of raspberry flavor. These cookies are fun, fresh and perfectly pink.

INGREDIENTS

for the raspberry sugar

¾ cup (90 g) confectioners' sugar

¾ cup (24 g) freeze-dried raspberries

for the snowballs

1 cup (128 g) macadamia nuts or pecans

2 cups (240 g) all-purpose flour

1 tsp ground cinnamon

¼ tsp ground coriander

½ tsp baking powder

¼ tsp salt

1 cup (226 g) unsalted butter, room temperature

¾ cup (90 g) confectioners' sugar

1 tsp vanilla extract

DIRECTIONS

To make the raspberry sugar, in a food processor, process the freeze-dried raspberries into a powder and pour into a small bowl. Add the confectioners' sugar and 3 tablespoons (12 g) of the raspberry powder into the food processor and pulse until very well combined. If you would like more raspberry flavor or a pinker color, add 1 additional tablespoon (4 g) of raspberry powder. Pour the raspberry sugar into a bowl and cover with plastic wrap (this helps prevent it from becoming gummy).

To make the snowballs, lightly toast the macadamia nuts in a small skillet over medium-low heat for 4 to 5 minutes, or until fragrant. Transfer the macadamia nuts into a food processor. Process until they are fine like the texture of almond flour. Cool slightly before using in the recipe.

In a medium mixing bowl, whisk together 2 tablespoons (8 g) of the freeze-dried raspberry powder, flour, cinnamon, coriander, baking powder and salt until well combined. In the bowl of a stand mixer fitted with the paddle attachment, beat the butter, sugar and vanilla on medium speed for 3 to 4 minutes, or until light and fluffy. Scrape the bottom and sides of the bowl as needed. On low speed, mix in the ground macadamia nuts until smooth and well combined. Scrape the bottom and sides of the bowl as needed. Mix the dry ingredients into the wet until well combined. Wrap the dough in plastic wrap and chill it in the fridge for 30 minutes.

Preheat the oven to 350°F (180°C). Line two large baking sheets with parchment paper.

Scoop 1-tablespoon (15-g) amounts of cookie dough into your hands, roll into balls and place them onto the baking sheets, spacing them 2 inches (5 cm) apart. Bake for 10 to 12 minutes, or until the edges are lightly golden brown. Cool the cookies on the hot baking sheets for 10 minutes. While the cookies are still slightly warm, roll them in the raspberry sugar. Cool completely to room temperature and roll them once more in the raspberry sugar if you would like a double coat.

maple-glazed apple cookies

makes 22 cookies

If I could pick one cookie to represent fall, it would be these spiced apple cookies. This recipe is perfect to make year-round but is an absolute must-bake in the fall. These cookies are chewy, fragrant, full of apple flavor and just incredibly delicious. Top them with a quick and easy maple glaze and you have fall in a cookie.

INGREDIENTS

for the brown butter

¾ cup (170 g) unsalted butter, room temperature

for the spiced apple cookies

2 cups (240 g) all-purpose flour

½ cup (56 g) almond flour

1 tbsp (9 g) apple pie spice

½ tsp baking soda

½ tsp baking powder

½ tsp salt

¾ cup (150 g) light brown sugar

½ cup (100 g) granulated sugar

½ cup (120 ml) unsweetened applesauce

1 large egg yolk

2 tsp (10 ml) vanilla extract

1 cup (125 g) shredded apple

for the maple glaze

1½ cups (180 g) confectioners' sugar

1 tbsp (15 ml) maple syrup

½ tsp vanilla extract

1 tbsp (15 ml) milk, plus more as needed

DIRECTIONS

Melt the butter in a heavy bottom saucepan over medium heat for 7 to 10 minutes, or until the butter starts to foam. Whisk continuously until brown bits start to form. Depending on your stove and saucepan, the entire process should take 10 to 15 minutes. Immediately remove the pan from the heat, and pour the brown butter into the bowl of a stand mixer fitted with the paddle attachment to cool slightly.

In a medium mixing bowl, whisk together the flour, almond flour, apple pie spice, baking soda, baking powder and salt until well combined. Add the sugars, applesauce, egg yolk and vanilla to the butter and mix until smooth and well combined. Stir the dry ingredients into the wet until just combined. Fold in the shredded apple until well combined. Cover the dough with plastic wrap and chill it in the fridge for at least 2 hours.

Preheat the oven to 350°F (180°C). Line two large baking sheets with parchment paper.

Scoop 2-tablespoon (30-g) amounts of cookie dough onto the baking sheets, spacing them 2 inches (5 cm) apart. Bake for 12 to 14 minutes, or until the edges of the cookies are set and lightly golden brown and the centers are slightly puffed. Keep the cookies on the hot baking sheets for 5 minutes before transferring them to a cooling rack to cool to room temperature.

While the cookies cool, make the glaze. In a medium mixing bowl, add the confectioners' sugar and stir in the maple syrup, vanilla and milk until well combined. Drizzle the glaze on top of the cooled cookies. Allow 20 to 30 minutes for the glaze to set before serving.

acknowledgments

Thank you . . .

To **Page Street Publishing**, for allowing me to bring a dream into reality. There is something truly magical about taking an idea and bringing it forth into the creation of a tangible book. Through each step of the process, you have been wonderful to work with. Thank you to Sarah, Meg, Laura, Will and the rest of the Page Street team.

To my **recipe testers**, your work in contributing to this book was invaluable.

To **my family**, both near and far, you have supported, listened and encouraged me countless times throughout my life. It means more to me than you can ever know.

To **my precious O + T**, you are the most beautiful souls I am blessed to love. Thank you for your laughter, love and constant calls for more cookies. You remind me every day of what matters most in this life.

To **my heart**, for guiding me, always.

To **you, the reader**. Whether you have known me for years or only stumbled upon this book by chance, your support is the reason I am able to do what I love. Thank you for inviting my recipes into your home.

about the author

megan neveu is a food writer, photographer and creator of the blog Olives + Thyme. She is an avid home baker with an insatiable sweet tooth. Her work is known for infusing fresh flavor combinations into classic and simple recipes. She lives in Texas with her two little cookie monsters.

Let me see what you're baking! Tag me in your cookie bakes on social media using the hashtag #SugarAndSpiceCookies

 OlivesNThyme

www.olivesnthyme.com

index